Discipline Over Punishment

Discipline Over Punishment

Successes and Struggles with Restorative Justice in Schools

Trevor W. Gardner

ROWMAN & LITTLEFIELD
Lanham • Boulder • New York • London

Published by Rowman & Littlefield
A wholly owned subsidiary of The Rowman & Littlefield Publishing Group, Inc.
4501 Forbes Boulevard, Suite 200, Lanham, Maryland 20706
www.rowman.com

Unit A, Whitacre Mews, 26-34 Stannary Street, London SE11 4AB

British Library Cataloguing in Publication Information Available

Library of Congress Cataloging-in-Publication Data

Names: Gardner, Trevor, 1975- author.
Title: Discipline over punishment : successes and struggles with restorative justice in schools / Trevor
    Gardner.
Description: Lanham, Maryland : Rowman & Littlefield, [2016] | Includes bibliographical references.
Identifiers: LCCN 2016023167 (print) | LCCN 2016032090 (ebook) | ISBN 9781475822250 (cloth :
    alk. paper) | ISBN 9781475822267 (pbk. : alk. paper) | ISBN 9781475822274 (Electronic)
Subjects: LCSH: School discipline. | Restorative justice. | Problem youth—Education. | Problem
    youth—Behavior modification.
Classification: LCC LB3012 .G37 2016 (print) | LCC LB3012 (ebook) | DDC 371.5—dc23 LC
    record available at https://lccn.loc.gov/2016023167

∞ ™ The paper used in this publication meets the minimum requirements of American
National Standard for Information Sciences Permanence of Paper for Printed Library
Materials, ANSI/NISO Z39.48-1992.

Printed in the United States of America

This book is dedicated to my son, Omari, who keeps me grounded in the possibility and necessity of a more just and equitable world;

And to the students at Hilltop High School (San Francisco), Thurgood Marshall Academic High School (San Francisco), East Oakland Community High School, City Arts and Tech High School (San Francisco), Envision Academy (Oakland), and ARISE High School (Oakland) who have taught me more than I could ever teach them about education, justice, humanity, and our way forward.

Contents

Foreword

The book you are about to read is a meditation on years of dedicated classroom practice. It is a reflection on the limitations of prevailing modes of discipline policies ushered in by the siren call for school safety and zero tolerance. The gap between the promise of safe schools and the life-altering consequences, for some of our most vulnerable students, is vast. These policies have revealed themselves to be an utter failure, making schools a less than safe space for many. Upon closer scrutiny, the very laws designed to protect children from violence have been a form of violence themselves, systematically revoking educational rights and opportunities, in most cases for little more than making an adult angry or "defying" their authority rather than committing crimes that endanger their classmates or school community.

This text is also a call to the community of educators, dream keepers, policy makers, and others to help imagine beyond our current crisis to envision a school system that is just in design and practice. One that values and cultivates the talents, interests, and innate brilliance of each and every child who walks through the schoolroom doors. It is a declaration that we can no longer countenance the systematic disenfranchisement of significant portions of our student population, our emerging majority. Enough is enough. We can do better; we have to do better.

Why restorative justice practices and why now? Restorative justice practices are nothing new; in fact, elements of these practices can be traced back to ancient times. They are currently gaining greater visibility, as increasing numbers of educational institutions are scrambling to identify and adopt more effective models for addressing issues of discipline and a healthy school climate. With scant evidence that zero tolerance approaches to school discipline actually deliver safer or drug-free environments, and mounting evidence that these practices are in fact discriminatory in outcome, there are additional incentives to alter policy and practice (Skiba et al. 2006; Skiba and Knesting 2014; Krisberg 2005; Fabelo et al. 2011). The real threat of lawsuits also makes these approaches more attractive.

After decades of get-tough policies, the pendulum seems to be swinging in the opposite direction. Some of this may simply be the vagaries of change, the episodic redirection in the cycles of school reform, but we would be remiss not to recognize the growing national confrontation with our legal system. An increasingly diverse legion of activists and concerned citizens are in the streets responding to police violence in communities of color. The killing of young black and brown bodies, seemingly too many to remember, seems endless and unrelenting. Many people have grown tired of the lack of legal accountability for the law enforcement agents and vigilante citizens who continue to surveil, control, and violate communities of color. The words, "To Protect and Serve," fall deaf on too many ears.

The emergence of critical texts, like *The New Jim Crow*, *Between the World and Me*, *States of Delinquency*, and the reemergence of classics such as *The Child Savers* and others have sparked a larger national conversation about fairness and justice. Research studies and investigations, such as the Ferguson report, suggest the racialized patterns of impact are in many respects extensions of past practices gussied up to be more palatable, but ultimately designed to deliver the same results. Revelations of patterns of prison sterilization and human-created catastrophes like the Flint, Michigan, water crisis remind us that the journey toward a truly inclusive and functional interracial democracy is ongoing.

The emergence of social media, the prevalence of handheld recording devices, and a growing presence of in-place surveillance cameras have allowed the average citizen and, in particular, disenfranchised communities to become producers of their own media. New avenues to curate and present alternative perspectives and imagery of lived experiences, too frequently denied or discounted in the mass media, have provided enhanced voice, visibility, and credibility.

In the critical race theory tradition of legal story telling, these new media tools democratize the opportunities to introduce alternative and counternarrative. Stories that demonstrate cries for justice are born out of lived injustice. Experiences that many Americans have been able to shelter from and ignore are more difficult to discount.

The demographic transformation of our nation also contributes to calls for reform. Indeed, it ensures this chorus for justice will continue. The current moment is ripe with possibility; there is real potential of developing coalitions across communities often at odds with each other. The emergence of movements like Occupy, #Blacklivesmatter, and similar organizations speaks directly to these possibilities. The very emergence of counter and alternative historical narratives make clear our histories are intertwined, as is our destiny.

To pique our sense of possibility and imagination, it might be useful to consider the reformation of school discipline policies as an act of transitional justice. Transitional justice refers to the set of judicial and nonjudicial measures that have been implemented by different countries in order to redress the legacies of massive human rights abuses. Many of the measures used in such processes attend to developing a comprehensive accounting of the events and factors that shaped the patterns of abuse. Among the goals most germane to implementing restorative justice practices in schools are halting ongoing abuses, preventing future abuses, preserving and enhancing peace, and promoting individual and national reconciliation.

In order to create a greater alignment between current educational practices and the function of democracy, it seems important to consider the history of public education and grapple with the context out of which it emerged in relation to what it was designed to do at the time of its inception and for whom.

Thomas Jefferson, the third president of our nation and principal author of the Declaration of Independence, was also an advocate for the common school. He believed the purpose of schools was to "rake a few geniuses from the rubbish." His words spoke to emergent beliefs about innate talents and abilities, but also ultimately about human worth. In *Notes on the State of Virginia*, he also stated, as a "suspicion only" that "the blacks are inferior to the whites in the endowments both of body and mind."

These ideas would shape inquiries into perceived human differences and, in turn, shape educational policy and practice. Ideas of lasting consequence were the assumptions that intellect was fixed rather than malleable and ascribed along lines of gender class and race.

Reams of data on disparate racial outcomes and new understanding about implicit bias and other forms of social conditions suggest these notions continue to shape policy and practice today (Skiba et al. 2002; Smith and Harper 2015; Losen and Gillespe 2012). If we are to create effective and inclusive schools, we will have to take history and its legacies into account in the same way a teacher might employ backward design when building curriculum. One single fact makes the need to reform apparent.

Increasingly, the students who inhabit classrooms across our nation represent the very populations of students historically deemed "unfit" and, as a consequence, only worthy of a separate but equal education. The history of segregation and isolation of educational opportunities provides us with ample evidence.

There is little profit in denying that the possibility of gaining a greater degree of membership in society through assimilation and the jettisoning of cultural markers of otherness offered to the masses of southern and eastern

European immigrants who flocked to our shores in the late nineteenth and early twentieth century was not possible for many immigrants and enslaved people in this country who bear the mark of Cain. No amount of assimilation or cultural divestment would make them "fit" enough for full membership. Similar narratives were hurled at these migrant masses from Europe until there was a commitment to make the very investments in them that allowed them to "become American." We will need to summon the political will to make these same investments in those who were systematically left behind or excluded from programs of collective uplift.

Sixty-two years down the road from the *Brown v. Board of Education* decision, schools are as segregated in most communities as they were at the time of the verdict. In places where more diverse populations exist, there is often segregation within schools. We must embrace the reality that these students are our students. These students represent our collective future.

Not all is lost. Schools are not actually broken. They do exactly what they were designed to do, and they do it well; it's just not what we need them to do at this point in time. Rather than identifying and sorting students, we need schools that inspire, engage, and uplift. In relation to discipline practices, we need policies that honor, embrace, and ultimately reconnect students while holding them accountable to the community for their actions.

Discipline should be educative, not punitive. Steps should provide consequences, but also opportunities to learn and alter behavior. When consequences occur absent of opportunities for growth or shifts in behavior, discipline is simply punitive and can be alienating. This work is really about investing in relationships and putting in place practices and procedures that honor the power of connection and community and that increase the likelihood, through structure and routine, that our best selves can be allowed to surface when conflicts arise.

Schools should not simply provide students with the skills necessary to be gainfully employed and positive contributing members of a society; they must also teach them how to engage meaningfully with the society in which they live. Restorative justice models that demonstrate ways to effectively resolve conflict can be powerful tools of civic learning. Such processes can help rebuild trust or faith in institutions for those on the margins or prevent students from feelings of alienation in the first place. Eradicating the legacies of racism and restructuring the institutions and systems that mark the "other" will be a challenge, but it is a challenge we must face nevertheless. We can ill afford to countenance the underdevelopment of vast swaths of human talent and potential.

Patterns of human wastage have always been policies of diminishing returns, but the cost of business as usual approach will have exponentially devastating consequences as our march of demographic transformation continues. Had we not forestalled this process of diversification through racially exclusionary immigration laws, we might have made these changes a long time ago, but the time is now. We have nothing to lose and much to gain. Tapping into the talent pool of underdeveloped and alienated youth could be a significant shot in the arm for us as a collective. Education is not an act of charity; it is an essential element of any healthy society.

Much of the research about the failures of zero tolerance discipline policies focus on urban schools and students of color, but it is important to consider that devaluation of certain segments of our population historically transcend our fairly narrow contemporary conversations of race. Historically, these taxonomies of otherness would have included poor whites, students with disabilities, queer students, and essentially anyone defined as nonnormative, so we must remain vigilant about the broader scope and legacies of these ideas and their current impact on students fitting these historically designated groupings. It is fair to suggest that meaningful and historically guided reform would necessitate the consideration of the wider sphere of influence of these ideas, if we are to construct new approaches to discipline that demonstrate the inherent value of all students.

The countenancing of injustice anywhere is corrosive to the larger goals and aims of a democratic society. We owe it to ourselves, and to our future, to develop a deeper historical comprehension of the patterns of institutional and structural devaluation and divestment of those deemed "unfit" that is necessary to enact the sort of comprehensive institutional reform required to redeem our school system, such that the predictability of inclusion and advancement have the same fidelity and continuity as today's patterns of exclusion and disenfranchisement.

The challenge we face is one of imagination; it is difficult to imagine beyond our current moment, but it is what we must do now. The world has never experienced a fully inclusive and functional democracy, but this is the opportunity we have. We have managed to come this far in spite of our past; to openly acknowledge and wrestle with it in search of a better, shared future is the work of democracy.

We invite you into this text and to join the conversation it is attempting to provoke. Be it an affirmation of your practice or a provocation, we encourage you to join the struggle for a more just and humane education system—one that will help us make true the promise of an inclusive and functional democratic society. The time is now.

Milton Reynolds
Program Associate – Facing History and Ourselves
Board Chair – Literacy for Environmental Justice

Preface

If you have come to help me, you are wasting your time, but if you have come because your liberation is bound up with mine, then let us work together.
—Lilla Watson

I begin every school year saying to my students, "this year you will teach me more than I could ever possibly teach you." They always laugh and dismiss my words, assuming I am joking or trying to win them over with a compliment on day one. But each June for nearly twenty years, I have reflected back and realized the truthfulness of this maxim. So much of what I know about teaching, about people, even about myself I have learned from the young people and families I have had the privilege of teaching and being in community with over the years.

As a middle-class white man who did not grow up in the communities where I have taught, this stance as learner has been crucial. I grasped early on the need to listen, look, and think with an open heart and open mind if I was genuinely going to serve the students and families with whom I worked. Over the years, the countless hours of reading educators such as Paulo Freire and bell hooks, studying pedagogy in critical inquiry groups, attending workshops, and engaging in professional development has taught me a great deal about the craft of teaching; but my students and families have shown me that great teaching must be rooted in a belief in the potential of their brilliance, and must be evidenced through work, dedication, and critical consciousness.

This book is a testament to all they have taught me. As a teacher and practitioner, I have developed important insights and experiential knowledge about how restorative justice functions in schools. Through positions of leadership beyond the classroom, and from dozens of books, conferences, trainings, and lectures, I have been able to merge my practical expertise with a theoretical and academic understanding of the power of restorative justice in changing classrooms, schools, and even lives.

Any limitations in this text grow out of this background as well—the reality that I have only taught where I have taught and learned what I have learned through my experiences in schools. It is not a dissertation on restorative justice. Nor am I a researcher in the field, gathering mountains of qualitative and quantitative data about restorative justice in schools. My insights and expertise emerge from the years of experience witnessing the transformative impact of restorative justice in schools.

As early as my first full year of teaching at Thurgood Marshall Academic High School in Bayview/Hunter's Point, one of the notoriously marginalized neighborhoods in San Francisco, I understood that traditional discipline systems in schools were failing students, some more than others. About five years into my career as a teacher, when I was finally standing on solid ground in my classroom, able to lean out the door and see beyond the walls of room 321, I began studying restorative justice practices as a vehicle for transforming student alienation and righteous indignation into engagement and empowerment. I came to see restorative practices as an essential tool for school transformation.

However, many educators with whom I spoke, both those working inside schools and in broader educational contexts, disagreed with my assessment. The reluctance of some teachers and school leaders was predictable. In schools, adults needed to be in charge and children needed to follow the rules. In their minds, this relationship of dominance and subordination was necessary for a functional and successful school.

But the doubt, and, in some cases, outright resistance on the part of some non-school-based educators, was both surprising and revelatory. "Restorative justice is a framework for responding to serious societal offenses and crimes, not a simple tool to be used on the playground and in the classroom," they would say. In other words, restorative justice is for serious matters and what takes place in schools is not that serious.

Except it *is* serious. While it may be true that a student being disrespectful to a teacher, getting into a fight, or bringing drugs to school does not carry the same weight as murder, apartheid, or many of the social ills restorative justice has been used to address in our broader society, the response to our young people in schools has life-shaping and life-altering consequences.

What I have come to realize, a truth I hope emerges through these pages, is that the transformative potential of restorative practices ranges from the micro-level of one-on-one interactions to the macro-level of rerouting the school-to-prison pipeline and improving life outcomes for young people. Implementing restorative practices in schools and classrooms is a win-win proposition. I know that it has made me a better educator and has changed the life paths of many young people with whom I have worked.

As my friend and colleague Milton Reynolds asserts in the foreword, we owe it to our students, their families, and our communities to "struggle for a more just and humane education system—one that will help us make true the promise of an inclusive and functional democratic society." Restorative justice is not a universal cure that will repair all society's ills or a superpower that educators can wield to bend schools and classrooms to their will. It is a set of beliefs and practices that, with the will, the investment, and the commitment, can be a force for justice and equity in our classrooms, schools, and beyond.

Acknowledgments

A multitude of people conspired to make this book possible. Foremost on the list are my mother and father, Jack and Linda, who have given me the gift of unconditional support for the past forty years; my brilliant partner and love-of-my-life, Shikira, who supports me and inspires me every day to do the real work to fight for a better world; and my son, Omari, who has taught me more than anyone else about what it means to be a teacher and a human being.

If you had asked me two years ago about writing a book, I would have laughed. I am a teacher. That is what I know and do. I feel comfortable in front of a classroom of students, but a blank page is daunting. The seeds that grew into this book were planted during my participation in a teacher-writing group convened by my friend and mentor Rick Ayers, a remarkable educator and writer. Anjali Rodrigues, another teacher and writer in the group, was a huge source of motivation and inspiration for me, as well as someone who offered me invaluable feedback on multiple chapters. I also want to give thanks to the other members of that group: Amy, Julia, and Tara.

Those original seeds grew through my participation in a restorative justice working group convened by another friend and colleague, Molly Schen, who works for Facing History and Ourselves, an organization that has contributed significantly to shaping who I am as an educator. She encouraged me to write an article about my experiences with restorative justice inside and outside the classroom and send it to her colleague Joan Richardson, editor of *Phi Delta Kappan* magazine. Joan supported me in getting that original article to publication, and that piece became the catalyst for this book.

Thank you to Sarah Jubar, my editor at Rowman & Littlefield, who reached out to me after reading that initial article in *Phi Delta Kappan* magazine and gave me the opportunity to share my insights and experiences through this book. She has been an attentive and encouraging voice throughout the process.

I am grateful to Facing History and Ourselves and the Innovative Schools Network for providing me a forum to share, explore, and build my work around restorative justice in schools. Jack Weinstein, Milton Reynolds, Kristin Botello, David Levy, and Meredith Gavrin have all been mentors and collaborators in this work for many years.

I could not have finished this book without the support, in the form of time, energy, and love, of my family and community. As a full-time teacher/instructional coach, writing during long weekends and late nights, their support has been invaluable. My brother and best friend, Jason, with whom I now teach, has been unconditionally supportive. My mothers-in-law, Michelle and Kay (my loudest cheerleader), have been a source of overwhelming emotional and spiritual support and guidance. Much love also to Nimka, Kamala, Kita, Bo, Sienna, Vivica, Tim, Frankie, and my entire community of friends and educators who have given me sustenance, encouragement, and motivation throughout the writing process.

I want to also recognize the educators, too many to name, who have supported, nurtured, challenged, and mentored me since I started teaching as a naïve and idealistic 22-year-old just out of college. Thank you: Patricia Keehan, Sandy Macaluso, Mark Salinas, Alec Perkins, Chuck Raznikov, Kevin Krasnow, Brian Frank, Allison Rowland, Robert Roth, Charmaine Ferrer, Lubia Sanchez, Daneen Keaton, Wayne Yang, Eric DeMeulenaere, David Philoxene, Ketia Brown, Jeff Duncan-Andrade, Cesar Cruz, Cliff Mayotte, Ben Rosen, John Kittredge, Elizabeth Lopez, Dennis Chaconas, and many more.

Several people have read chapters and given me feedback on various aspects of the book. Thank you to Sparky, Kita, Jenevra, Mark, and Naomi for thoughtful insights and genuine investment in the project. Your voices are definitely reflected in these pages. Eran DeSilva has been an amazing friend and editor, reading multiple chapters, providing thoughtful feedback, and investing in the success of this book as though it was her own.

I want to give deep appreciation to my friend and mentor, Dr. Tony Lepire, who has been my most profound and loving supporter since I took his course sixteen years ago while I was in the teacher credential program at San Francisco State University. Not only has he edited and given me extensive feedback on most of the book, he has taught me much about what it means to be a dedicated, compassionate, and skillful educator in a complex profession.

Finally, I want to show deep gratitude for all of the students and families whose stories are captured in these pages, especially Raymond, Abel, Luz, CJ, Josh, Stephanie, Freddy, and Gibran, whose voices are heard throughout. It has truly been a gift to learn from them and grow with them over the years.

Chapter One

Philosophy and Practice

Toward a Restorative Approach to Student Discipline

REFERRAL, SUSPENSION, EXPULSION: THE PUNISHMENT ETHOS

Schools can be incredibly conservative institutions where change comes slowly. Nowhere is this evidenced more clearly than in the realm of student discipline. Anyone truly aware of the state of discipline in schools today must be indignant about our current state of affairs.

According to the Civil Rights Project at UCLA, about 3.5 million K–12th grade public school students were suspended in the 2011–12 school year, nearly half of whom were suspended at least twice. If you add up the total number of days students were suspended that year, you reach an aggregate of over 18 million days of lost instruction. Further, this total is complicated by the disparities in suspension rates based on gender, ethnicity, and poverty. Add this all together, and you arrive at one of the most troubling issues weighing on public education today.

Since public schools have been in operation, not much has changed in terms of how we attempt to control and moderate student behavior. Detentions, suspensions, and expulsions—at most schools across the nation these persist as the fundamental tools used to bend students to institutional will.

The fact that schools continue to rely on escalating punitive consequences and that we have not created and implemented, on a systemic and structural level, alternative and more effective methods as the primary means of disciplining students represent a tragic failure of innovation and forward thinking in public education. What makes this lack of progress particularly troubling is that punitive methods have not actually proven to be effective, on the

1

whole, in changing the behavior of students. Punishment alone, especially using removal from the classroom or the school as the primary form of punitive consequence, does not work.

Furthermore, as the introduction to this book discusses, the consequences have been and continue to be grave, especially for poor students, African American and Latino students, and students with disabilities. However, confronting this ethos of punishment that persists in our schools, we do see models of effective school discipline that transform behavior and improve academic success for all students.

This book is an exploration of how several educators have attempted, with varying levels of success and effectiveness, to implement some of these alternative discipline models in their classrooms and beyond. These practices have taken multiple forms and have been put into effect in different ways, depending on expertise and context, but the common thread is their rootedness in restorative justice as a founding principle for establishing school culture and classroom coherence.

DEFINING RESTORATIVE JUSTICE

Similar to the way critical pedagogy provides an alternative to the traditional "banking" model of education, restorative justice gives us an alternative framework for the one-size-fits-all punitive model of school discipline. Though restorative justice is an expansive concept encompassing various principles and practices, the fundamental tenet is that it "engage[s] those who are harmed, wrongdoers, and their affected communities in search of solutions that promote repair, reconciliation and the rebuilding of relationships. Restorative justice seeks to build partnerships to reestablish the mutual responsibility for constructive responses to wrongdoing within our communities" (Center for Restorative Justice – Suffolk University).

It is important to specify here that this book will define restorative justice in broad terms. As we are exploring ideas of restorative justice and, more generally the pursuit of more just treatment of students in the context of schools, some of the practices we describe do not fit into a strict definition of restorative justice. In many ways, the methods outlined in these pages are *simply good teaching*. Relationship building; meeting students where they are; starting with questions before jumping to judgment; building structures for respectful student-to-student conversations; these are all solid pedagogical practices in themselves. And they are also key aspects of a restorative justice framework in schools because they prioritize relationships, collective responsibility, and differentiation as pathways to student success. This is an orientation toward teaching that has worked for the educators and schools that fill the pages of this book and for an increasing number of schools that are working to put restorative justice into practice in myriad ways around the country.

The body of literature focused on restorative justice in society and in schools grows every day. In education, restorative justice has become one of the most common tools called upon in today's current school reform. Just in the past year, several excellent and insightful texts addressing school discipline, restorative justice, and the school-to-prison pipeline have emerged (Laura; Nocella II, Parmar, and Stovall; Rios; Wadhwa). However, few of these texts provide insights into the day-to-day implementation of restorative practices from the perspectives of educators currently working inside schools and classrooms. This book attempts to provide that vantage point as honestly as possible, in a way that exposes the possibilities and successes as well as the barriers and struggles of doing this work.

TOWARD A RESTORATIVE JUSTICE FRAMEWORK IN SCHOOLS

Given its effectiveness, why is a restorative approach to discipline not *the* common framework being used in schools around the country today? Certainly, despite adequate data pointing to the failure of punishment as an agent for behavioral change (Greene; Roth, Assor, Niemiec, Ryan, and Deci), this tendency toward punitive consequences is not isolated to schools; it reflects, as stated above, a broader ethos of punishment in our society. Ultimately, we must address this punitive culture on a societal level. This is an issue rooted in our system of capitalism that breeds class division, racism, social reproduction, and the maintenance of class hierarchy. But it is not within the scope of this book, nor the expertise of its authors, to build a case for the alleviation of this ethos in our society as a whole.

Schools, however, because they are such highly structured and controlled spaces, and because offenses in schools are generally more moderate than those faced in the criminal justice system, are a suitable place to start to explore and implement practices that provide an alternative to our punitive culture and to begin to alleviate the consequences wrought by it. Schools provide clear opportunities for engaging in the process of shifting toward a restorative justice paradigm.

Furthermore, if we can find successful ways to engage and build community with young people while they are still in school and, at the same time, offer them a sense of community and a feeling that the adults surrounding them truly care about their well-being, then fewer of them will be pushed toward behaviors that force them to confront the criminal justice system later in life.

Our schools purport to serve everyone. All young people in this country are required by law to attend school until they are at least sixteen years old (in some states this age has been raised to seventeen or eighteen). So schools must find ways to empower our young people and set them on paths of transformative possibility, not to replicate the societal repression and criminalization that makes the United States the most punitive nation in the world.

The statistic that takes up the most space in this river of punishment is our incarceration rate, which at over 700 prisoners for every 100,000 citizens, according to the American Psychological Association (2014), is the highest out of any nation in the world. However, there are many smaller tributaries of punishment contributing to what the American Psychological Association calls our "Incarceration Nation." The school system, as it currently operates, is undoubtedly one of those tributaries.

However, participation in the restorative justice process in school, in its many forms, teaches students that they are responsible for learning from their mistakes and fixing the problems that impact their communities, a skill set that ultimately extends beyond the school building and has the potential to stem the flow of the river of punishment.

To reiterate, it is both problematic and unrealistic to place the burden of such a profound societal change on the shoulders of our education system. Our schools are increasingly tasked to address and "fix" many of the broader social ills that we struggle with, whether it is the scourge of drug addiction, the negative influences of the media and technology, or the inequities created by falling wages. However, the microcosm of schools does provide a space of opportunity for the exploration of what is possible. At their best, schools can and should model the challenges and the possibilities of the "real world."

This chapter will discuss the interplay of philosophy and practice, two elements essential for establishing successful structures of restorative justice in schools.

THE PHILOSOPHY: A UNIVERSE OF OBLIGATION

A restorative philosophy is based on the vision of a school as a community of learners in relationship together, who owe responsibilities to one another due to that relationship. It assumes an understanding of discipline more connected to its etymological Latin root than to the popular definition in education today, within which it is essentially synonymous with consequences for actions that transgress a set of expectations set by school officials. The word discipline comes from the Latin verb *discere*, meaning "to learn," and the noun *discipulus*, or "pupil." Therefore, in a restorative context, discipline involves the process of placing oneself in the position of a pupil, a reflective position in which learning from one's actions is the goal. The restorative element, as stated above, involves the understanding of oneself as a member of a community to which one has a connection and a responsibility.

This philosophy is not, in itself, new. In fact, according to J. Braithwaite, restorative justice was "the dominant model of criminal justice throughout most of human history for perhaps all the world's peoples" (2002, 8). Many of the beliefs espoused by restorative justice practitioners today are rooted in indigenous American and African ways of knowing (McCaslin 2005, 7). They focus on the collective as opposed to the individual and aspire to achieving balance and harmony instead of effecting retribution.

This is not to say that the restorative justice practices we see today, inside and outside of school, closely reflect the indigenous traditions in which they are rooted. The new wave of restorative justice as it has manifested since the 1970s in places such as Canada, the United States, and Western Europe, and as it has been attempted and implemented in schools, has been adapted to fit its various historical, political, and social contexts.

Helen Fein, a historian and sociologist who specializes in the study of genocide, human rights, and collective violence has developed the concept of the "universe of obligation" to help students understand the idea of obligation to community. Fein describes the "universe of obligation" as "the circle of persons toward whom obligations are owed, to whom rules apply and whose injuries call for [amends] by the community" (Holocaust and Human Behavior xviii). This concept helps elucidate the philosophy of restorative justice, a philosophy that must be at the foundation of a model of restorative discipline in schools.

If a restorative justice discipline model is going to be successful, educators at a school must hold certain beliefs about the purpose of discipline and the importance of relationships in creating a positive and transformative learning environment for all. They must also believe in the development of an authentic sense of community as a necessary element in the education of young people. In other words, they must hold their students, and ideally their colleagues, in their "universe of obligation" and treat them accordingly.

The following eight principles represent several key beliefs compiled by schools in the Bay Area where restorative justice is being successfully implemented.

KEY BELIEFS OF A RESTORATIVE JUSTICE DISCIPLINE MODEL IN SCHOOLS

1. There Must Be a Foundation of Community

The meaning of the word *community* is frequently left vague, undefined, or ill-defined when used in the context of schooling. Many of the distinct elements that build a sense of community will be discussed below as aspects of the restorative justice discipline model, but with such an expansive term, it is important to begin with a clear general definition. Community in a school includes, but is not limited to, a shared sense of purpose, agreed upon values toward which all members are committed to working, a sense of responsibility to other members, and a duty to work toward the safety and well-being of others.

Note that these elements are all described as acts of becoming. It is unrealistic to assume that, even in the healthiest and most stable communities, these components are all being fully realized at all times. Rather, community is the outcome of a continual commitment to the realization of these elements.

In order for a restorative justice approach to work, a school must have established a basic sense of community to which students, staff, and parents feel a sense of connection and responsibility. One of the most common pitfalls of efforts to implement restorative discipline practices is that schools have not first done the work to build this sense of community and obligation, resulting in empty or meaningless consequences.

The absence of community is perhaps also a critical reason why restorative justice is not implemented more frequently in schools. Schools that do attempt a shift toward restorative discipline often make the mistake of trying a few restorative practices, such as circles or public apologies, with the belief that these will magically shift their entire school culture. Then, when they do not experience the shift for which they had hoped, they turn back toward traditional punitive discipline practices.

This same dynamic is also why the wholesale adoption of "packaged" restorative justice models by districts or schools rarely finds success. Restorative justice can be one aspect of a transformation in school culture and the creation of community but it cannot, by itself, realize such structural changes. In order to require that students and staff restore their membership in a community, that community must first exist and encourage a sense of obligation. All members must be committed to engaging in the process of healing and transformation.

2. Discipline Should Transform Behavior, Not Just Address Individual Actions

Two basic beliefs undergird the punitive justice paradigm that dominates school discipline policies today. The first is that students who make bad or harmful choices deserve retribution. The second is that responding to offenses with equally harmful consequences will keep the offender from making the same choices again, consequently changing her or his behavior.

A restorative justice paradigm believes something fundamentally different; namely, that students who make bad or harmful choices should be held accountable to their actions through a process of reflection, communication, and action that makes right the harm they have done, not through punishment.

When we rely on harsh and retributive actions, including the traditional trio of detain, suspend, and expel, it only serves to further marginalize young people who, regardless of their life circumstances, are already going through a time of transition that is challenging socially, emotionally, and physiologically. This is not to say teachers and school leaders should avoid demanding high expectations for student behavior and discipline.

When students transgress classroom expectations and school core values in significant ways, the response needs to be equally significant and serious. But, in order to transform behavior, the response must also come from a place of genuine care for the individual student and the well-being of the community. This is also why trust is crucial. Young people only receive critique and consequences if they come from someone with whom they have a relationship of trust.

Furthermore, an increasing amount of research is informing us that our students' brains are not fully developed until they are in their early twenties and that the parts of the brain responsible for impulse control and planning are among the last to mature. It is essential for us to take this into consideration in the context of school discipline policies.

3. Harm to an Individual Is Harm to the Community

Restorative justice holds that the community is paramount to the individual. If students get into a fight in front of school, or come drunk to the Halloween dance, or turn over a desk in anger, the entire school community is impacted. If a teacher belittles a student by telling him to shut up, the entire class may be traumatized. If a principal unfairly accuses a group of students of graffitiing the bathroom, community trust is broken. Therefore, a restorative response must take into account the various different stakeholders who were impacted and the consequence must respond, in some way, to these stakeholders.

The response to a victim or perpetrator of an act of bullying, for example, will of course differ from the response to the bystanders. The restorative process will guide the consequences and outcomes for each community member involved. The belief that sets restorative discipline apart from punitive discipline is that all community members involved were affected and, therefore, must be involved in the process of healing and moving forward.

4. Participation Is a Choice

Connected to the principle "There Must Be a Foundation of Community " is the understanding that all people impacted by the incident, especially the perpetrator(s) and the victim(s), must choose to participate in the restorative process. Participation should never be forced or coerced. For victims, this might entail waiting days, weeks, or even months before they are ready to engage in a process of healing and transformation.

But what about community members who commit an act of aggression, who disrespect others, or who otherwise violate school rules and expectations? At schools with strong community, this is rare, which is why the principle above is important. But it does happen. Many young people, especially when difficult emotions are involved, basically demand the punishment option because they fear the reflection and responsibility-taking that a restorative process requires. In that case, schools and teachers have no choice but to resort to more punitive tactics.

Still, even the punitive response should maintain the dignity of the student and should be related to the violation. A student should never receive a more severe punishment for refusing to participate, in a given moment, in the restorative process. Wherever a student stands in the school environment, the goal of a discipline policy is to bring them closer to a sense of community and belonging, not to alienate them further due to poor choices they have made.

5. Shifting the Power Dynamic

Schools are not literally prisons, but there are obvious reasons why this analogy is so frequently drawn. There are few institutions where the power dynamic between those who are serving and those who are being served is so one-sided. At most schools, being accused of fighting, stealing, cheating, or being defiant or disrespectful by a teacher or administrator is equivalent to a conviction, especially at schools that serve mostly low-income students whose parents have limited political or social capital.

Students know that they essentially have no rights at these schools and that the only power they can wield comes in the form of their immediate physical or verbal response to an accusation, usually in the form of talking back, raising their voice, or some other display of frustration. After all, if they know they are going to receive a referral, detention, or suspension, why not earn it?

Effective restorative justice discipline models shift this power dynamic and guarantee students a voice in the process, allowing them to tell their side of the story and even suggest appropriate consequences. It also requires that all people involved in an incident show up and take responsibility. Too often, students are forced to take full responsibility and endure the punishment of a transgression, but adults who may have played a part in causing or perpetuating the incident are left alone. Restorative discipline transforms this power imbalance by requiring the same investment of all community members.

6. We Must Attend to the Root Causes

No student comes to school as an empty slate. Physically, intellectually, emotionally, socially, culturally, even politically, students have spent years in a process of becoming before they arrive at our classroom doors. Part of the reason why punitive discipline models do not succeed in changing student behavior is that they focus only on the actions and choices of students in a given situation without much attention to the context or factors outside of that moment.

Instead of digging into the roots of the issues that cause the defiant behaviors, schools cut away at the branches, which quickly grow back. We find ourselves dealing with the same behavioral issues with the same students in cycles of struggle and resistance, which ultimately lead to suspensions and expulsions and the origin of the school-to-prison pipeline.

Instead of expending so much time on purely punitive responses that only address behaviors, a restorative approach to discipline seeks to address and influence causes, which include anything from academic frustration to students dealing with trauma due to the death of a loved one. A restorative response can be as simple as a teacher responding to a student outburst with a sympathetic "Are you okay?" instead of a reactionary "What is wrong with you!" And it can be as complex as a reentry circle attended by ten to fifteen concerned community members for a student who is returning from a month in juvenile hall.

7. Equity Is Not Equality

When it comes to school discipline, equality does not mean equity; nor does it translate to justice. This principle is difficult to communicate to students, especially younger students with their incredible attention to fairness. But it is necessary if we are going to find ways to meet all students where they are at and empower them toward academic success.

Isaiah, whose grandmother recently died and who is experiencing PTSD from other trauma in his life, requires a different level of support than Alexis, who has a safe and supportive home life and is emotionally stable and healthy. Students are complex individuals with extremely different needs and relational skill sets, and we must implement discipline policies that respond accordingly.

Most punitive discipline policies do not provide the space to respond differently to the myriad of students and situations school experience every day. In fact, oftentimes teachers and administrators are forced by these policies to take actions they know will further harm their students. Zero tolerance policies are the most damaging example of practices that force educators to treat all violations of school rules or expectations equally, regardless of the context or root causes.

A restorative model, on the other hand, inherently seeks to understand the complexities of students and why they make the choices and take the actions they do—and responds accordingly. The goal of restorative justice is to produce equitable outcomes, not simply to respond equally to all situations.

8. All Students Want and Deserve the Opportunity to Learn

The correlation between incidents of student discipline (usually resulting in suspension) and academic success is self-evident. When students get in trouble often, they feel a lower sense of academic identity. When students are punished for missing class and missing school, they are less successful in their classes. The fact that punitive discipline policies lead to increased student failure for our most vulnerable students is evident. When we remove students from the classroom, for an hour, a day, or a week, we are taking away their opportunity to learn.

A restorative justice paradigm holds the belief that all students both want and deserve to learn, even those students who struggle and challenge us most. This may be difficult to see or retain when a student is cutting school or wreaking havoc in a classroom, but it is a key principle in a restorative philosophy. What follows, then, is that our classroom practices and discipline policies must do all they can to keep students *in* the classroom.

Chapters 2 through 6 delve more deeply into several of these key beliefs and provide specific examples of what they look like and how they play out in the classroom and beyond.

MYTHS AND MISCONCEPTIONS

At this point in the discussion, there are always educators who push back and argue that restorative justice in schools takes away the authority of the teachers and administrators and amounts to low expectations for student behavior and a chaotic school culture. While a poorly implemented restorative justice discipline model can, indeed, result in these issues, a successful one results in the opposite. The list that follows is meant to dispel a few of the misconceptions about restorative justice in schools. Restorative discipline in schools does **not** mean:

Students can do anything they want and get away with it.

Not true. While a restorative discipline framework responds differently than punitive measures, it does not change *which* behaviors and incidents are addressed. Cheating, defiance, drug use, graffiti of school property, biting, kicking, and fighting are still not permitted.

Holding low expectations for student behavior.

Just the opposite. Which is a more rigorous response to a student disrupting a classroom: being sent to spend the rest of the day in the dean's office on in-school suspension or being asked to read a letter of apology to the class and hold a restorative conference with the teacher? A restorative response is both rigorous and relevant because it engages students in consequences connected to their transgression. Furthermore, it requires reflection not only about their individual actions but also how their actions impacted their classroom or school community.

Punitive measures are thrown out.

This depends on our interpretation of the word punishment. It is true that restorative justice turns away from punishment as a response to harms done, but this certainly does not imply the absence of consequences. Most of the time restorative consequences involve a more serious "punishment" than punitive repercussions in that students perceive these consequences as more difficult to fulfill. Additionally, if students refuse to engage in a restorative process, then punitive measures must be in place to hold them accountable to their actions.

The student is always right.

The student is always given voice and treated with respect, and this, unfortunately, is enough to make some educators uncomfortable with the restorative process. But there is a significant difference between empowering a student to share her or his perspective and that student being right.

It takes away the authority of teachers and administrators.

This misconception is only true to the extent that it removes the teacher or administrator as the only authority in a student discipline situation. Restorative discipline does shift the balance of power in that it eliminates the silencing of students created by punitive models of discipline and creates the space for student voice. Additionally, because restorative discipline draws much more heavily on the involvement and accountability of the school community, teachers and administrators are consequently held accountable in a way they are not when they are operating in isolation.

FROM PHILOSOPHY TO PRACTICE

Belief in the power of a restorative approach is not enough. Belief is a necessary element, but not adequate for establishing an effective system of restorative discipline. Schools also need a concrete set of skills and practices to serve as the skeleton that holds the system together and keeps it from caving under the weight of all that schools are tasked to do in our society.

Understanding restorative discipline as a unique skill set is crucial because it requires schools to acknowledge the need to develop these skills in order to ensure the success of their students. Most of the time school culture and discipline are things that are taken care of by the dean, administration, and, increasingly, security guards and school resource officers. Beyond focusing on classroom management, minimal time and resources are provided for school-wide staff development around school culture and discipline.

If restorative discipline is going to be successful on a systemic level at a school, all members of the school community need to develop the skills and practices necessary to embody the principles outlined above.

Not all schools practicing restorative discipline are the same, and they certainly are not using restorative practices in the same way. At a small charter school of 300 students and 15 teachers, a whole-school approach that requires several days of staff training and curriculum for every classroom might be the right approach. At a large comprehensive public school with 2,000 students and 150 teachers, it may make more sense to begin with a small cohort of teachers and students implementing restorative practices.

If the shift toward restorative discipline comes from the teachers, then classroom-centered practices should be the starting point; whereas if the leaders have more investment in these new practices, weaving them into the school-wide discipline policies makes more sense. A robust Student Justice Panel might be the cornerstone of the restorative justice discipline model at a school with strong student leadership, while circles might be the main level of restorative power at another site. There is no all-inclusive model that officially designates a school a "restorative justice school." Additionally, schools are in different places in terms of their readiness to shift toward a restorative model, and this must be taken into account as well.

Though the challenge of shifting educators' beliefs about discipline to a more restorative approach involves a deeper level of reflection and change, transforming practice can be equally as formidable.

PRACTICES THAT RESTORE

One challenge that complicates the transition to a restorative justice discipline model is that, like most things in the education world, there is no manual or set of guidelines for making this change. What follows is not meant to be a comprehensive list of restorative discipline practices in schools, nor is it a one-size-fits-all blueprint.

What is true is that the more of these practices and structures schools are able to put in place, the more robust and effective their discipline model will be. They can be thought of as pillars that hold up the extremely heavy and multistoried structure of school culture and student discipline. One or two pillars will not provide much support for this structure, but the more pillars a school adds, the more sturdy it becomes and the more robust and transformative the restorative model stands.

The list below is a summary of multiple restorative discipline practices and structures that we have found to be effective at various schools around the country.

1. Core Values

Though not specifically a restorative justice structure, the establishment of a set of school-wide, agreed-upon core values provides the foundation for school culture and student discipline. Schools almost always have a clear mission statement and set of rules, which can be found somewhere in the student handbook, the school website, or even sometimes on posters that adorn the hallways and classroom walls. But these are not the same as core values, which are aspirational and give language to a school's academic, social, and professional goals for their students. If rules and academic expectations tell students what they are supposed to do or not do at a school, core values communicate who we want students to *be*.

In its fourth year of operation, East Bay Charter Academy, in Oakland, California, recognized they had various structures and expectations that spoke to students about how to behave and achieve academically. School rules outlined acceptable behavior, and leadership skills and the graduation portfolio defined academic success. But there was no standard for character and identity that provided guidelines for who we wanted our students to be on their way to academic achievement.

The question often surfaced: is academic success enough? Are we successful if we graduate students who make it through college and find professional and financial success if they go on to contribute to the injustice and oppression in our world? The answer was "no" and the core values were developed largely as a response to these questions.

In the end, after an extensive democratic process that included the voices of staff, students, and parents, East Bay Charter Academy decided on five core values:

Discipline – We discipline ourselves so that no one else has to.

Growth – We are committed to lifelong learning and personal growth.

Community – We work hard and take responsibility for the success of all members of our community.

Justice – We are empowered agents of change for social justice and equity.

Respect – We seek to see the best in each other and treat one another with dignity. We give respect in order to get respect.

These core values reflect the unique community of East Bay Charter Academy, and their dreams and aspirations for their students. Though the content of the core values is obviously important, of equal substance is the *process* of establishing these values and finding ways to make them live and flourish at one's school. Oftentimes when visitors would come to visit the school or when students were speaking at events outside of school, the core values would be the first thing talked about in terms of what made East Bay Charter Academy the school it is.

2. Student Justice Panel

A Student Justice Panel or student court, as it is sometimes called, is a body that places students in charge of handling the response to specified discipline issues. See chapter five for a detailed description of the Student Justice Panel.

3. Circles

Restorative circles or peacemaking circles are probably the most common restorative practices being utilized in schools today. The purpose of a circle is to bring together the community members who are concerned about a particular student or student issue or who have been impacted by an offense in order to collectively come to a restorative solution. A circle might consist of only a few people, a perpetrator, victim, and a teacher, for example, or it could be comprised of fifteen or more participants, including family members, advocates, and peers. The size of the circle as well as the amount of time allotted to the circle process is determined by the needs of the situation. Circles are held for a wide range of issues, from welcoming back students who have been absent from school due to incarceration to addressing issues of bullying on campus.

Led by a trained facilitator, each participant passes a "talking piece" and has the opportunity to share her or his experience and perspective without interruption. The process encourages open communication in a safe space that feels supportive to all people involved. By listening attentively to all perspectives and experiences, the goal is to strengthen relationships and a sense of community while still coming up with a restorative solution to the issue that prompted the circle process. If the circle is a response to a specific harm, outcomes include holding the offender(s) responsible for their actions and for restoring the harm they caused to the victim and the broader community.

Restorative circles are also powerful tools for healing and rebuilding community after a particularly challenging or traumatic experience in the classroom.

4. Conferencing

Conferencing is similar to the circle process with significant overlap between the two practices. Conferencing is more strictly focused on conflict resolution and generally only involves the community members who are directly involved in a given incident. This process involves a teacher, administrator, counselor, or even a peer mediator who brings together the parties involved in an incident with a clear focus on resolution and responsibility. Whereas the circle process can be long and elaborate, providing ample time to engage all perspectives and dig into the roots of an issue, conferences can be more brief and resolution-oriented.

One clear example of conferencing is the "4 Options Model" outlined by Ron and Roxanne Claassen in their excellent text *Discipline that Restores*. Formulated specifically for use in the classroom, the 4 Options Model is a tool to be used when students are unwilling to cooperate with teacher requests and reengage in on-track behavior. It requires students to choose one of four conferencing formats to resolve a conflict, two of which are facilitated by an outside person and two of which involve only the student and teacher (Claassen 2008). Ultimately, the 4 Options Model is a way to try to give students agency in the midst of challenging classroom situations while still holding them accountable to rigorous expectations.

One critical dilemma schools operating under a restorative paradigm face is the limitation of time. Restoring takes more time than punishing. Conferencing can be a tool that respects the value of restoring while understanding the need to be efficient with time and resources.

5. Peer Mediation

Peer mediation is a form of conferencing that empowers trained students to lead their peers in the conflict resolution process. Student mediators lead their peers in reflection and problem solving in order to keep minor incidents from turning into more significant transgressions. Peer mediation is often used to quell rumors and trash-talking before it escalates into more serious conflict.

One of the powerful aspects of peer mediation is that it forces students to find ways to solve their own problems instead of relying on staff to do so.

6. Public Apologies

The public apology has the potential to be a powerful tool in the repertoire of a restorative justice discipline model, but it can also be extremely punitive and even harmful, depending on how it is utilized. In a restorative context in schools, the public apology is not about shaming a student into changing her or his behavior or punishing a student through public embarrassment. Rather, a public apology involves the communication of responsibility and account-ability to one's community and the recognition that harm done to any member of the community is harm to the entire community.

Public apologies can be structured in different ways. They might be addressed only to one classroom where an offense occurred, to a specific group of people during a restorative circle, or to a whole-school community at an assembly or gathering. Still, the essential features of a public apology must include: 1. Recognition of how the offender violated the core values or community expectations; 2. Taking responsibility for the harm to the individual victim (if there is one) and the community; and 3. Commitment to addressing and rectifying the harm done. Obviously, the public apology must be (and must be perceived to be) sincere and authentic for it to be effective.

The third feature of the public apology is particularly important because a student will feel much more obligated to commitments made to the entire community than she or he might be if those commitments are only made to a teacher, principal, or other staff member. But this public acknowledgment also shifts school culture in that it asks fellow students to step up and support the offender in maintaining her or his commitments.

7. Student Support Groups

Though student support groups are not unique to schools that embrace a restorative discipline paradigm, it is crucial to include them on this list because they provide a necessary restorative option when students make choices that harm themselves and the community. Restorative discipline in schools is difficult partially because of the limitations of the consequences schools have available to them. If not referrals, suspensions, and expulsions, schools find themselves asking, then what? Student support groups can be one element of that "what."

One of the many reasons students respond negatively to punitive discipline is that they do not understand the connection between their transgression and the punishment they receive. Inappropriate language results in a detention. Defiance results in a referral. Cutting class results in a suspension. Possession of drugs results in expulsion. Regardless of the violation of school expectations, the response is similar and almost always involves either holding students in a room for a given period of time or removing them from class and school altogether. The only factor that changes is the length of time a student is detained or suspended. So, regardless of the root causes of a transgression, students are punished in a similar way.

Student support groups contribute to a restorative justice discipline model because they allow for consequences that match the offense. If a student comes drunk to school, one of his consequences could be attending a substance abuse group run by a staff member or outside counselor. If a student bullies her peers, she might be required to attend a young women's identity development group. If a student uses homophobic language, the student could be asked to attend Gay/Straight Alliance meetings. These are just a few examples of the utilization of student support groups to reinforce a school's restorative justice discipline model.

8. Adult Reflection

The final practice we discuss focuses on adults and staff culture as a pillar of a restorative discipline program. This practice is valuable for two reasons. First, educators sometimes need to engage in a restorative process when they have committed offenses that harm the school community. For a restorative model to work, staff must hold themselves to the same expectations to which they hold their students. Second, the work of building and maintaining a strong and positive classroom environment and school culture can be incredibly taxing. Schools and school leaders need to create the space for their staff to be together in positive and nurturing ways.

As far as prioritizing positive adult reflection, given the time restraints of schools and the reality that there are always more things to do than the time and resources to do them, this practice is ignored by most schools. However, one school in Oakland, California, that has successfully implemented adult reflection is United for Change Charter School. At United for Change, one three-hour professional development session per month is a dedicated time for staff to focus on their own health and well-being as professionals and human beings.

Chapter 9 will go into detail about the restorative justice process for staff and the need to hold ourselves, and each other, accountable to the same expectations as our students.

CONCLUSION

If at this point you are feeling overwhelmed, it is okay. Keep a few things in mind. First, change comes incrementally. The shift to a restorative justice discipline model is literally a revision of a paradigm that has dominated schooling for generations. Magnify that by the fact that schools in this country are institutions that operate inside the most punitive society in the world and you realize the monumental nature of the task. Therefore, it is essential to integrate restorative justice in a way that feels viable and through which results can be seen and experienced by the staff and students.

This might mean starting with only a handful of teachers who already embrace a restorative philosophy and building from there. Or it could entail weaving restorative beliefs and practices into your professional development for a year before putting it into effect with students. Whatever your process, if you attempt to take on more than your school community is ready for, you will most likely go the way of many others that "tried" restorative justice but found that it did not work for their community.

Next, do not forget that it takes both the philosophy and the practices to build a successful restorative justice discipline model. If you go hard on the beliefs about restorative justice but have no concrete structures or practices to support this stance, your school will most likely become a space with little accountability, where students are held to low expectations because you want to meet them where they are at without pushing them to continually grow.

On the other hand, if you jump straight to the implementation of structures and practices without the critical mass of community members having adopted the key beliefs, you will create more conflict and resentment than you will heal. As restorative justice takes root more deeply in the realm of educational initiatives, more resources and programs emerge that claim to be able to transform schools into models of restorative justice. It is crucial to keep in mind that restorative practices are not a silver bullet, nor a prepackaged solution to a school's discipline issues. Schools must transition thoughtfully, in both philosophy and practice, toward a restorative paradigm.

Finally, remember that restorative work is about transforming lives. Throughout this book you will hear the stories of young people struggling to navigate the complex demands of schools, neighborhoods, and communities that ask them to be and do many different things. Go to college. Be an independent thinker. Follow the rules. Blaze your own path in life. Be safe. Join this gang. Pass this test. Obey your parents. Listen to what your teachers tell you. Drink this. Try harder. Trust authority. Sit down. Stand up. Be yourself. Follow in these footsteps. For even the most healthy and disciplined young people, life in schools is a labyrinth with right and wrong choices at every turn.

How do conversations and real outcomes change when we begin with the premise that to make errors or mistakes is to be human? In schools, a restorative justice discipline model is to recognize this reality while presenting children and adults with choices that enable growth and save lives.

Chapter Two

Restorative Discipline and Classroom Management

Seeking to Understand First

Chris was a new student at East Bay Charter Academy. On day one of school, he sauntered into Mr. Warren's fifth period U.S. history class all laughter and disregard, trying too hard to make a point. He was one of three new students among a close-knit class of juniors who had been together since ninth grade, but his confidence, at least on the surface, concealed the fear and insecurity he carried. When his talking continued right through the bell and into the beginning of class, Mr. Warren knew a power struggle was looming on the horizon.

Having taught this same group of students for the past two years, as their critical literacy teacher in ninth grade and their world history teacher in tenth, Mr. Warren had largely moved beyond these types of direct challenges. By their junior year, his students knew him, and his expectations, like they knew their own work habits. They knew that when the last student rushed through the threshold and the door closed, it was time to learn. They knew to have their writer's notebooks out and pens ready as soon as they sat down. They could repeat his "go-to" teaching mantras, like "discipline yourself so no one else has to," without prompting. Students and teacher had built a relationship of mutual respect with rigorous expectations of each other. But this was not the case with Chris, a detail that led to the experience and restorative process that begins this chapter.

When Chris's chatting continued at full volume after Mr. Warren brought the students to attention to write down the purpose and homework, a routine that begins every class, his first thought was, *has this kid forgotten about where he is and what he is supposed to be doing?* Fortunately, Mr. Warren's tone did not reveal his annoyance and a simple behavior correction, along with the conspiring voices of a few other students who had the teacher's back, was enough to get Chris focused and on point—this time.

But the pattern continued. Every day, fifth period began with Chris chatting to one student or another, often a little too garrulously to be incidental. He would wait for Mr. Warren to directly call him out and ask him to get focused before bringing his conversation to a leisurely halt. After two weeks of the same behavior, followed by the same in-the-moment response on the teacher's part, he decided it was time to draw a clear line with Chris, and one that would last longer than a single class period.

The two went through their quotidian dance at the beginning of the period, but when Chris started chatting again several minutes into the period as Mr. Warren was teaching, the teacher walked toward him in obvious frustration and ordered, "Chris, I need you to move over there (pointing to a seat across the room and away from his friends) and stop talking while I'm talking. Is that too much to ask?"

Ending the statement with more of an exclamation point than a question mark, Warren chose to let his emotions take the lead in his response to Chris's behavior. The student grumbled about not being able to move because he couldn't see from the other seat, and Warren responded by escalating the situation even more, "Chris, I need you to move your seat right now!"

Now, Mr. Warren has been teaching in the urban high school classroom for sixteen years. He is clear that every classroom management textbook asserts the danger of engaging in power struggles with students in front of their peers, but he also believes there are situations that merit this kind of direct confrontation—and, at the time, he thought the Chris routine was one of those moments.

Chris's reaction to the demand surprised him as much as it continued to anger Mr. Warren. He simply closed his eyes and ignored his teacher, whose patience had been entirely exhausted. After another ignored request, Chris responded, "Don't talk to me right now. I'm praying to my higher power."

Mr. Warren, perceiving the student's response as joking insolence, replied with his own disrespectful words, "If you can't listen to a totally reasonable request, then you need to get out, now."

Mr. Warren, in visible aggravation, followed his student out the door where the tension continued to escalate. Chris was clearly not in a mood to discuss his behavior, and Warren's frustration was not helping the situation, so the teacher drew one of the final arrows in his classroom management quiver.

"I don't have time for this. You need to go to the dean's office and see Mr. Younger right now."

Chris agreed, but said he needed to get his backpack out of the room first. When Warren blocked his way and told the student he could not go back in the classroom, Chris exploded, "If you don't get out of my way I'm gonna punch you in your face!"

Fortunately for both teacher and student, Chris realized that he had gone too far and overstepped even his own boundaries. Backpedaling, both physically and emotionally, Chris's next words were a little calmer.

"Can you just get my backpack, so I can go up to Mr. Younger's office?"

Mr. Warren retrieved the backpack from inside the classroom and sent Chris on his way, already beginning to reflect on the multiple mistakes he had made in one of the most tense five minutes of his teaching career.

HOW DID IT GET TO THIS POINT?

Once his emotions had subsided and the teaching day came to a close, Mr. Warren had a chance to reflect—and realize that the teacher he had become in the classroom with Chris was the antithesis of the educator he imagined and wanted to be. *How did I ever let the conflict get to that point?,* he thought to himself, as he began to consider his next steps for following up.

This moment of looking back and reflecting is pivotal in helping teachers to shift toward a more restorative classroom practice. Too often, especially given the myriad of interactions a classroom teacher has in a given day, several of them inimical and challenging, this moment is lost or forgotten. The teacher simply moves on, leaving the responsibility of disciplining the student to the dean or some other outside force who is somehow supposed to "fix" the offender and send them back to class the next day ready to learn.

Such expectation elucidates a fundamental problem with the traditional punitive practices that continue to stand as the bedrock of most school discipline models: the belief that punishment changes behavior and that disciplining a student is someone else's responsibility. A growing body of research on adolescent behavior and punitive justice contradicts this belief (Lewis 2015; Roth et al. 2009) but, in this arena, most schools, educators, and society as a whole continue to place belief above data in deciding policy.

Fortunately, as a teacher who believes positive relationships and trust are essential to a student's willingness to learn, Mr. Warren's reflections stay focused on his role in the Chris incident; he cannot avoid his responsibility in undoing the harm he has caused Chris, his fifth period U.S. history class, and himself.

To be sure, the responsibility of creating this destructive situation was not entirely the teacher's, but he knew any way forward that would genuinely transform this destructive dynamic with Chris would have to emerge from him. Even if Mr. Younger was able to "fix" Chris and get him to take responsibility for his actions, the student's feeling of bearing the entire blame for the mutually disrespectful incident would hinder any chance at a productive and trustful relationship moving forward.

This is a common dynamic in schools: Adults have all the power, and students must be obedient and respectful—even when they are right (and righteous) in the face of injustice. This is the dynamic that leads to so many students blowing up over incidents that begin as small.

After many years of schooling, students have learned that the teacher's word is taken as truth, and their perspective won't matter. Being told to move seats or getting a detention for repeatedly talking can often lead to screaming at a teacher, storming out and slamming a door, or throwing a fit because that is their only source of power, or simply because their sense of futility just cannot take any more.

They have seen models of struggle—from "World Star Hip Hop" to the contentious political climate—that value temper tantrums and threats of violence to win one's point. Surrounded by a society that combines suppression of free expression with a climate of hostility in which everywhere they turn—television, the internet, police and gangs in their neighborhoods, and, sometimes, their own households—they find aggression and force beings used as tools to address all problems. And they employ these same tools competently when they find themselves powerless in classroom situations.

When there is no space for discourse and no acknowledgment of the righteous indignation of young people, as Langston Hughes declared over sixty years ago, like dreams deferred, they explode.

Conversely, restorative classroom practices bring with them a fundamental shift in the power dynamics inside the classroom and the school building. They require the recognition that in order to maximize learning, students, teachers, and other members of a school community are bound in a relationship with one another, one that involves corresponding obligations from all parties (Zehr 2002). In contrast, traditional punitive discipline policies in schools typically only require the student to fulfill her or his obligation to be respectful and obedient while the teacher is assumed to be inherently correct.

This was not a power dynamic Mr. Warren was interested in leveraging, which is why he followed up with Dean Younger that same afternoon to ask about the consequences of Chris's referral and how the follow-up conversation went. Mr. Younger explained how Chris calmed down easily and was able to articulate his role in the incident, reflecting on what he could have done differently. However, when asked to meet with Mr. Warren the next day and apologize, Chris was reluctant and backpedaled into "I didn't do anything wrong" mode. The meeting with the dean ended with Chris begrudgingly agreeing to apologize (or risk being suspended) but clearly not meaning it.

When it came out in Mr. Warren's follow-up with the dean that Chris had threatened to "punch [the teacher] in the face," Mr. Younger's tone changed, and he immediately suggested the maximum five-day suspension for the threat. Again, this moment represented a critical opportunity to embrace a restorative response to the destructive incident.

The effortless response would have been to simply send the student home for five days in order to "learn his lesson" about how to respect teachers. Ironically, the only lesson generally learned by this suspension, a punishment that, according to the UCLA Center for Civil Rights, was meted out nearly five times as frequently for African American students as their white or Asian counterparts, would have been a reinforcement of the understanding that students are powerless in the face of school discipline policies and teacher directives.

It is important to acknowledge the seriousness of threatening a teacher or any member of a school community with physical violence. It is an absolutely unacceptable behavior and one that requires firm consequences. But under the paradigm of a restorative approach to discipline, consequences do not equate to punishment, which is why Mr. Warren requested that, instead of being suspended for five days, Younger set up and facilitate a conference that would decide the appropriate consequences—and what each needed of the other in the classroom.

Mr. Younger agreed, and added that he had already spoken with Chris's parents, who wanted to come in and meet with his teachers to discuss their son's previous experiences in schools as well as some strategies that had worked (or not worked) with him in the past. A conference involving Mr. Warren, Chris, and his parents was set up for the following day.

Chris and his mother settled into the worn leather couch in the dean's office with Mr. Younger sitting at his desk across from them. When Mr. Warren arrived, he pulled up a chair adjacent to the couch, forming a rough "U" shape so that everyone was facing each other in the conversation. Chris's body language, slouching into the couch, hat pulled low to cover his eyes, told Warren that he was expecting to be criticized and reprimanded. He had clearly been stuck in this situation myriad times before and he was not expecting his voice to be heard or respected.

The first words out of the teacher's mouth immediately shifted this dynamic.

"I want to start by saying I'm sorry for how I handled the incident in our class yesterday. I know I escalated the conflict by speaking to you disrespectfully in front of other students. I was frustrated and, although I think you could have handled it better, too, I shouldn't have come at you the way I did."

Chris immediately came out from hiding under his baseball cap and looked Mr. Warren in the eye and said, "I just don't like being told where to sit. In my last school, they always forced me to sit in the back of the class; even if I didn't do anything, they made me sit in the back. I can't sit back there."

At this point, Mr. Younger paused the conversation and asked both Chris and Mr. Warren to back up and share their perspectives on the incident from the beginning. During Chris's explanation of the events, he reflected several times on experiences at previous schools that had led to him getting in trouble or incidents during which he was treated disrespectfully by teachers, principals, or other school personnel with no recourse and no mechanism for being heard other than raising his voice or "going off" on someone.

When he got to the part about the teacher not letting him pray to his higher power, Chris's mother jumped in to explain further, "Chris has always had problems focusing in school, since he was small. We have tried so many things, and one of the techniques his counselor has suggested is that, when he is feeling himself starting to get angry or ready to go off, he closes his eyes for ten seconds and prays to his higher power. It's something we encourage him to do."

LISTEN, LOOK, FEEL, RESPOND

The restorative conference with Chris and his mother was a success. First, it kept Chris in school and learning instead of spending an unstructured five days at home—a routine he was thankful to avoid. Additionally, the conference, only two weeks into the school year, left Chris with the emerging understanding that East Bay Charter Academy did things differently than the schools that had acted *on* him in the past—and Mr. Warren was not simply another authoritarian white teacher who understood nothing about where he was coming from.

In only a half hour, teacher and student learned enough about each other and built enough trust and goodwill to begin a foundation that would continue to grow throughout the year. The decision to restore (or, more accurately, to begin building) the student-teacher relationship through a conference instead of punishing the offender with suspension shifted not only the dynamics of their classroom interactions, but also Chris's overall perception of the school community.

Mr. Warren left the conference feeling rejuvenated. *That is the kind of teacher I want to be*, he thought as he rushed to begin teaching his next class period, remembering a crucial piece of advice he had received from a mentor several years back: relationships with students are earned, not given.

What Mr. Warren had forgotten, as do so many teachers every day, every class period, and every interaction with challenging students, is to begin with listening, looking, and trying to understand before moving on to feeling and responding. One of the simplest, yet most effective restorative responses inside the classroom is to begin with the questions "Are you okay?" or "What do you need right now?" when a student acts out inappropriately.

Mr. Warren had let his escalated emotions shape his reaction to Chris's insolence, which led to the situation going from zero to "I'm gonna hit you in your face" in only a few minutes. He missed the opportunity to let Chris know he was attempting to see, hear, and understand him in that moment, an error that, fortunately, led to a transformative end product in the conference, but one that could have been avoided with a simple question.

Even though this classroom disruption had a positive outcome, in terms of classroom management, it is always better to transform and prevent destructive behavior than it is to escalate and, later, restore it.

INTERFERING WITH TEACHING AND LEARNING

One of the most insidious claims to arise in the No Child Left Behind era is the assertion that "nothing interferes with teaching and learning." This mantra is proudly displayed, in bold letters, at the front of classrooms across the country. While the spirit behind these words reflects a necessary urgency— *classroom learning time is crucial and every minute counts*—the underlying message reveals a dangerous myopia in regards to the lived realities of the students who walk into our classrooms every day.

So many experiences interfere with teaching and learning. Chris's memory of being forced to sit in the back of class at his previous school because he was perceived as a troublemaker before he even walked through the door interferes. The anniversary of Rickey's mother dying of a drug overdose interferes. Asiay getting kicked out of her mother's house over winter break interferes. Jessica's feeling of failure because her younger sister just dropped out of high school interferes. And on and on.

By saying *nothing* interferes with teaching and learning in schools invalidates and erases the very real experiences that young people carry with them into the classroom. A 2010 report by the Justice Policy Institute found that up to 34 percent of youth in the United States had experienced at least one traumatic event such as physical or sexual abuse, neglect, war, or community violence and up to 46 percent of young people had reported being witnesses to violence (Adams 2010). Such occurrences are even more frequent for poor youth and youth of color. These are the experiences that unavoidably contribute to who they are and how they experience the world, and which, most certainly, shape their ability to learn at any given moment.

The term "restorative justice" is an overarching term that describes a philosophy and set of practices that puts harm done, accountability for that harm by the wrongdoer, and repair of that harm at the center of the problem solving, involving the stakeholders in the matter (Thorsborne and Blood 2013). The missing piece of this definition is a recognition that, in the context of schooling, for many students, a great deal of harm has been done to them (by their families, their neighborhoods, their poverty, police officers who are supposed to protect them, and the like) long before they enter into relationships with their schools, their teachers, or their classes.

This is not an attempt to dismiss, simplify, and objectify the rich and complex lives of urban young people, as does the insidious culture of poverty narrative. Rather, it is a willingness to understand and believe the root causes of behavior, roots that, in most cases, find their origin far deeper than the foundation of any school building.

A more appropriate term to describe the aspect of restorative justice that involved relationship building, one that Mr. Warren uses in the work with restorative discipline practices, is *preventative justice*. Preventative justice begins with the recognition of depression, trauma, neglect, violence, poverty, and oppression as an enduring force in the lives of many school-aged youth and, consequently, the need to meet students where they are at and to listen, look, and understand what is going on with them in moments of conflict.

Preventative justice in the classroom looks like teachers beginning with the question, "Are you okay?" when students act out. It looks like investing in relationship building with struggling students in the same way teachers invest in rigorous lesson planning. It looks like establishing structures like the Student Justice Panel, which will be amplified later in the book, so that students know they have a voice and support in matters of discipline and behavior.

Mr. Warren, despite his classroom experience, failed to approach Chris with the advice he had given to many schools and teachers throughout his tenure. He did not listen, hear, and understand first; he did not practice preventative justice.

If he would have, he would have learned that asking Chris to move to the back of the room would trigger him, or that when Chris said he needed a moment to pray to his "higher power," he was not disrespectfully blowing off the teacher's orders. Mr. Warren would have been the teacher he wished to be instead of the teacher who deserved being sent to the dean's office for his behavior.

At East Bay Charter Academy, an Oakland charter school of 400 students and 20 teachers, interactions like the one between Chris and Mr. Warren play out multitudes of times every day. The power to shift school culture, student engagement, and, ultimately, student learning through restorative and preventative discipline practices is profound.

BUT WHAT ABOUT THE CONSEQUENCES?

At this point, readers may be saying to themselves, *wait a minute—a student threatened a teacher with physical violence. The conference may have made both teacher and student feel better, but what about the real consequences for his actions?*

Good point. Consequences are essential in holding all community members responsible for creating and maintaining a safe and respectful space of learning. But consequences are not analogous to punishment, which is what most people mean when they use the term consequences.

As a consequence for his actions and for breaking the school's core values of *Respect* ("We seek to see the best in each other and treat one another with dignity. We give respect in order to get respect.") and *Community* ("We work hard and take responsibility for the success of all members of our community."), Chris had to face his teacher and take responsibility and apologize for his behavior. (Later, he also wrote a letter of apology to Mr. Warren.)

The next day, Chris apologized to the class for disrespecting them and their learning. (Mr. Warren also apologized for his role in escalating the situation.) Additionally, Chris was required to help Mr. Warren in his classroom after school for a week, completing whatever tasks the teacher needed help with. It is important to note that all of these required consequences asked the wrongdoer and the harmed to turn *toward* one another and engage, as opposed to turning away and removing the wrongdoer from the community he harmed and to which he was obligated.

In contrast, Chris could have been "punished" by the dean suspending him from school for five days.

Most advocates of punitive discipline policies provide justification with empty expressions like "students need to be punished so they learn their lesson." But what would sending Chris home for five days have accomplished? What lesson would he have learned?

He would have fallen further behind in school, apparently learning that students who transgress school expectations do not have the right to learn. He would have grown more aggravated with both his new school and his new history teacher, increasing the likelihood of East Bay Charter Academy becoming another link in the chain of schools that failed to engage and educate this young black man—a pattern with perilous consequences for thousands of students just like Chris. Finally, he would have learned, yet again, that his voice was inconsequential and that school demanded his obedience instead of his intelligence, and his silence instead of his empowerment.

Restorative discipline practices require an investment that may seem demanding and burdensome. Indeed, holding a restorative conference, convening a healing circle, or organizing a Student Justice Panel requires more time and resources than indiscriminately suspending or even expelling a student. But should schools not be asked to hold themselves, in regards to their disciplining of students, to "high expectations" in the same way they are held to these expectations academically?

Just as asking students to complete some form of multilayered performance task is more rigorous than taking a multiple choice test, restorative discipline practices are more rigorous, for both students and school personnel, than punishments.

Restorative justice is the manifestation of high expectations in the realm of school discipline, in the truest sense of the words. To discipline a student is to assist him to learn from his actions or, as Morrison and Vaandering insightfully define it in their article "Restorative Justice: Pedagogy, Praxis, and Discipline," discipline is "a means for nurturing human capacity rather than a method of managing others" (Morrison and Vaandering 2012). It must be understood that the immediate investment in preventing and restoring greatly outweighs the long-term cost of flushing more students down the school-to-prison pipeline.

Chris is an example of the efficacy of the restorative strategy. It would be naïve to assume that one restorative conference, in the wake of a history of acting out, silencing, and marginalizing that stretches back into elementary school, would magically transform Chris's entire relationship to school. However, for the rest of the school year, when Mr. Warren asked Chris to stop his side conversations and focus in class, the student listened.

More often than not, in fact, Chris became a strong support for the teacher, reminding other students to get on point or "discipline themselves so no one else has to," another one of Warren's favorite maxims. For Mr. Warren, Chris's presence in class was an important reminder that looking, listening, and working to understand his students before behavior issues even arose was the most powerful tool he had in ensuring his classroom would be a space of liberation and rigorous learning for all.

Chapter Three

Meeting Students Where They Are and Building Relational Ecologies

THE FRANKY INCIDENT

Franky is a brilliant young man, insightful, charming, and creative. He is the kind of student who is both liked and respected by all, teachers and peers alike. He has been a shining star in Mr. Warren's English and history classes since tenth grade. However, Franky's relationship with school has not always been a positive one. He is a strong-willed and independent student with a clear sense of moral responsibility—one that does not always align with the expectations of teachers and school officials. This fact has resulted in far too many trips to the principal's office and has ultimately developed in him a sense of what can best be described as righteous indignation toward school.

Franky's righteous indignation manifests in different ways. It could be as simple as him exhorting students to "be quiet" when a shy student is trying to speak in a talkative classroom. Or it could look like him "talking back" when a teacher has said something he believes is disrespectful. Ultimately, it is not uncommon that Franky gets sent out of class or called into the dean's office for some perceived transgression.

But when Franky's teachers at East Bay Charter Academy, including Mr. Warren, received an e-mail, in the middle of the afternoon, that he was going to be suspended for five days (the maximum time allowable in California) and possibly expelled from school, they knew that something serious had happened and that someone needed to get involved and, if necessary, to advocate for Franky before the situation got out of control.

Here is what happened: during his second period math class, Franky was opening his backpack to pull out his work when the teacher saw an object that looked like a knife at the bottom of his bag. She immediately called the

29

assistant principal to come take the student to the office. Within minutes, the principal had sent Franky home and communicated to him and his mother that his possession of a knife was grounds for a recommended expulsion. At the very least, according to California law, she said she was required to remove him from school for a sentence of five days. End of conversation.

The problem with the zero tolerance attitude, and other heavily punitive discipline policies, is that the "conversation" should be so much deeper and more complex than the principal's mere adherence to the "policy" or the law as she interpreted it. The conversation should not begin with the moment Franky walks in the door and end when he leaves for the day. Meeting students where they are at requires schools and educators to be in conversation with the fullness and complexity of each individual they serve; each one, rich with culture, family, history, language, and struggles that must be engaged and understood if we wish to empower young people to use education to transform their lives.

This moment with Franky gives us an illustrative text through which we can examine the intricacies involved in school discipline. Franky lives in deep East Oakland, a neighborhood known more for its gangs and violence than for its rich culture and revolutionary spirit. Franky is not large or daunting. He is barely five feet six with his Nikes on, and it is hard to find him without a playful smile stretching across his face. However, as a young Latino man, Franky, because of the color of his skin, the clothes he wears, and the swagger in his walk, is under constant threat of being attacked on his path to and from school. It is simply the reality of his surroundings.

It does not matter that he is a natural intellectual, that he is the student most likely to sacrifice his own well-being for the benefit of his peers, or that he loves to get out of the city and camp under the stars. In a neighborhood where being "young and Latino" carries so much symbolic weight, despite the myriad layers underneath, Franky is a target. Walking home from school he has been jumped, threatened, and certainly scared more times than he is willing to admit. So he came to school carrying a knife for protection and self-defense. And on this particular day, Franky made the mistake of being careless.

To be clear, in his math class Franky did not brandish the weapon or use it to threaten another student. He was not bragging about the knife with other students. He simply had it in his backpack—a violation of school policy, for certain—but far from a serious threat to other students or the school community. So when his teachers got word that Franky might be expelled for making a choice he believed to be necessary for his safety, several of them came to his defense.

Mr. Warren recalls this moment and the complexity of moving to act on Franky's behalf. He was not sure how to respond. The student did, after all, bring a knife to school, an act which he did not want to find himself trying to defend. But he also knew that he saw a different Franky than the principal, or at least that the school discipline policy, allowed her to see. He knew that he needed to insert himself into the situation in order to at least shift the punitive momentum that had built up. Mr. Warren knew that this was a potentially life-changing moment for Franky, as well as a potentially transformative moment for the school.

Both the immediate and overbearingly punitive response to Franky's transgression and the process that followed elucidate several key learnings about a restorative approach to discipline. These lessons must compel us to meet students where they are at when they enter our school doors if we genuinely wish to support them in reaching both our academic and behavioral expectations.

A FALSE OPPOSITION

One of the most common challenges with implementing a system of restorative discipline in schools is the clash, sometimes manufactured and sometimes very real, between maintaining a safe school community and supporting the well-being and growth of individual students. "We cannot sacrifice the whole class/group/school in order to save this one student" is often the refrain of teachers and administrators who are struggling with difficult behavior issues—a situation exacerbated by the structural limitations and systemic burdens schools endure, as discussed in greater depth in chapter 8. This clash is further aggravated by the conflicting "rules" of schools versus the neighborhoods in which many of our students live.

In Franky's case, school policy deemed him a threat to the safety of his peers. In our punitive world of school discipline, he should, therefore, be removed. The principal in this case claimed to have no freedom to respond differently, as she was following state education code. Zero tolerance. Consequently, zero space is allowed for the discussion of the context of the situation. There was no room for Franky's reality and his need for safety. There was no inclusion of the student's character and the fact that, in his four years at East Bay Charter Academy, the most unsafe behavior Franky had exhibited was talking back to teachers or minor verbal altercations with peers. He had not been involved in a single incident involving violence or harm to another member of the school community.

If space had been created for Franky to speak his truth, the principal would have at least learned a great deal more about his reality. This is not to say the principal or the school could have changed the material conditions of Franky's life that made him feel like he needed to carry a knife, but it would have at least been an acknowledgment of his reasoning in making this decision—a much more productive starting place for solving the problem than sending him away for five days or shipping him off to another school.

However, ultimately, as in most situations involving student discipline, the student's voice was silenced and his experience of the situation rendered inconsequential in service of the "greater good" for the school community as a whole.

"THE GREATER GOOD"

For many teachers and school leaders working under overwhelming conditions with minimal support, removal seems to be a reasonable solution to the perceived obstacle to learning—removing the "problematic" students so the rest can take better advantage of their educational opportunities. Within the punishment-centered model of discipline, this tactic makes a lot of sense. It is almost intuitive: remove the harmful actor and the class/group/school will function more smoothly. The problem with this traditional approach is that it sees the students as disconnected individuals in a neutral classroom space so that removing one or even a few "problematic" students would lead to a net positive impact on the entire class. But is this effective? And, if so, at what cost?

Jason, a tenth grade student, who was ultimately thrown out of East Bay Charter Academy due to constant behavioral issues, provides a powerful counter-narrative to the "removing the problem students" theory of school discipline. Despite his kindness, humor, and intelligence, by many measures, Jason was, for teachers, the most difficult student in the tenth grade. He received multiple warnings per day from his teachers for his inability to stop talking or stop drumming on his desk. He was kicked out of class several times per week, a pattern so consistent that he had taken to simply walking out of class when he could not sit still or felt like a conflict was approaching. School administration, teachers, and even other students were beyond frustration with Jason and could not figure out how to support him toward success in school.

Eventually, Jason was placed on a contract that outlined certain behaviors he would have to follow and supports and accommodations he would receive in order to get on track academically. The requirements of Jason's contract were not unreasonable for most students, but for Jason, the agreements were beyond what he was able, or at least willing, to uphold. He was the perfect example of a brilliant young man who would flourish given the right environment, circumstances, and supports. The school building, the classroom walls, and the traditional discipline policy at East Bay Charter Academy, however, were not able to force Jason into compliance and, therefore, academic success. So, ultimately, Jason broke his contract multiple times and was kicked out of the school.

Although a genuine effort was made to put supports in place to help Jason meet the school's expectations, it was not enough to meet him where he was at, with all his talents and eccentricities as well as challenges and struggles. It was clear from the beginning that his fate was written and that the contract was a way to justify getting rid of a "problematic" student who simply took up too much space in his classrooms and whom the school did not have the expertise or the will to serve.

The assumption behind the exiting of the myriad Jasons in our schools is that *they* are the problem and the reason for the dysfunction of our classrooms and schools. Remove these individuals and things will automatically begin functioning more smoothly.

The fallacy in this thinking is that despite the highly individualistic culture perpetuated by most schools, students are not isolated mechanical parts working separately toward individual academic success. Rather, students are connected through a powerful network of relationships that go far beyond what we see inside the school building every day. They see themselves in Jason.

They, too, experience the struggle of sitting for seven hours per day in plastic chairs engaged in work that often feels to them uninspiring and irrelevant. They have had parents yell at them the night before, have stayed up until 3 a.m., and have struggled to keep their eyes open through the day. They have wanted to jump out of their seats in the middle of class or been so hungry that it is impossible to focus. And almost all of them have lost friends and family to violence and had to come to school the next week and function as though their hearts were not torn wide open.

So, for example, in the U.S. history class, when Jason is kicked out for continually getting out of his seat and acting a fool, his peers, even those who might be annoyed by his antics, empathize with his struggle to navigate an institution that is deeply challenging and unaccommodating to individuals like him. When the teacher removes Jason from class, especially if done in a way that is disrespectful or harsh, he loses a bit of his earned authority in the class. This can result in needing to rely more on his positional authority, thus leading to more conflict in the future. His peers understand Jason's right to an education, and they feel the injustice of him being denied this right by being kicked out of class or removed from school.

Furthermore, because the students in class watching Jason get kicked out every day know that, in many ways, they are him or, at least, that he too has every right to his education, they inevitably lose trust in the teacher or the principal who is taking away Jason's right to this education. Ultimately, in an attempt to make the classroom or school space more focused, productive, or safe by removing the "problematic" student, the choice to remove even very challenging students makes it more difficult for students in the class to trust the teacher in the future and causes harm to the community as a whole.

"NOT A FIT"

Jason is not an isolated case. In fact, for students like Jason across the nation, his experience leans toward the more positive end of the spectrum in that the teachers and school leaders at East Bay Charter Academy genuinely cared about Jason and, within the limitations of their punitive discipline system, wanted to support him. Still, though the details of the process vary, the purpose and outcomes are as consistent as the concrete onto which we release our students.

Ta-Nehisi Coates (2015) illuminates the devastation of this cycle of exclusion in his letter-to-son-essay *Between the World and Me*, "Fail in the schools and you would be suspended and sent back to [the] streets, where they would take your body . . . those who failed in the schools justified their destruction in the streets" (33). In fact, this removal, for many, is the initial phase of the school-to-prison pipeline.

Sometimes intentionally malicious toward these students and sometimes stemming from a genuine inability to serve some of the most marginalized students in our schools, the pipeline often begins with the belief that the given school or classroom is "not a good fit for him or her." This excuse is used frequently to justify eliminating the Jasons and the Frankys in our schools. By the time many students, especially poor African American and Latino boys, have made it to high school (many like them are pushed out before even reaching the ninth grade), they have been given the message that they do not belong many times by multiple teachers and schools.

Jason, for example, came to East Bay Charter Academy as a tenth grader after being kicked out of three other high schools already. As they move from school to school, our students in most need of support and restoration compile records of negative behavior that feed prejudice about them before they even enter the doors of their new school.

This giving up on so many of our young people who struggle most in school represents the worst kind of punishment because it essentially tells students they do not have a right to their education. Without saying it, the message to students is "maybe school is not for you," and, especially for many urban students of color, the alternative path is prison.

A DIFFERENT PATH

This repressive picture does not have to be the only answer—and is not the case when one finds oneself in schools or classrooms operating under a restorative paradigm, which understands all community members are connected in an ecology of relationships (Morrison and Vaandering 2012). Researchers Brenda E. Morrison and Dorothy Vaandering (2012) examine how restorative justice relies on the "'soft' power of relational ecologies" rather than the "'hard' power of the [law and/or code of conduct] of the institution." In this context, all students, even those who are responsible for harm or disruption, must be considered a necessary part of the solution. The goal of maintaining the community is paramount.

In Mr. Warren's classroom at East Bay Charter Academy, one assertion that attempts to build such a community is that there is not only a single teacher in the classroom. Rather, everyone in the classroom is there as both teacher and learner and, though the teacher holds a unique place in terms of knowledge, expertise, and authority, genuine and deep learning will only occur when every class member takes responsibility and ownership and participates in teaching the others what she or he has to offer. Consequently, removing a student from the classroom results in removing one of the teachers, a necessary component to maximizing the learning of all.

In Ms. Garcia-Marquez's ninth grade English class at East Bay Charter Academy, every class begins with In Lak'Ech, a Mayan precept invoking the shared humanness of every person in the room. The recitation goes as follows:

IN LAK'ECH

Tú eres mi otro yo.
You are my other me.
Si te hago daño a ti,
If I do harm to you,
Me hago daño a mi mismo.
I do harm to myself.
Si te amo y respeto,
If I love and respect you,
Me amo y respeto yo.
I love and respect myself.

In Lak'Ech provides a powerful example of the work that must be done to establish the foundation for a practice of restorative justice in the classroom. When teachers build a culture of mutual responsibility, dignity, and even love in their classrooms, then the expectations are that all members of the community will work to do whatever it takes to support one another. Removing a student from this environment, whether temporarily or permanently, requires much more serious consideration and justification than a traditional classroom focused on individual success and accountability.

Under this paradigm, the removal of any student, even the most marginalized or challenging, results in a disruption to the ecology of the classroom and harm to the community of all classmates and the teacher.

Such a stance may force many teachers and school leaders to acknowledge that punishment and forced removal can be harmful. Even if a student, through his choices and actions, has hurt the classroom or school community, responding to harm with harm is not an effective way to maintain a safe community. Nor is it an effective means of creating a positive and transformative space for learning for which all members of the community bear responsibility.

This brings us back to Franky and Jason. The restorative principle of meeting students where they are at requires the recognition that we bear responsibility for helping to heal harm done to members of our community, even if that harm was not caused by us. If we are truly committed to serving and supporting all students, then we are compelled to find ways to meet their needs and work beyond the traditional structures of a school system that expects all students to show up ready and prepared to learn in the same way.

THERE ARE NO WEEDS

Is the expectation that we support all students toward educational success, including continually searching for restorative ways to build their membership in community, a potential setup for disappointment? Or failure? Let's compare teaching to a few other professions—parallels that provide some thought-provoking insights into the relationship between restorative discipline and the dilemma of the support of the individual versus the good of the group. Let's talk about doctors and lawyers.

Doctors occasionally watch their patients die before their eyes despite their greatest efforts. Lawyers sometimes lose cases despite putting forth their strongest arguments. Sometimes there are just factors beyond our control that make success impossible. In schools and classrooms across the country, despite incessant political rhetoric to the contrary, this acceptance of failure has become the norm.

It is true, in other professions 100 percent success is not an expectation. Nor should it be a practical expectation in public education, given the fact that we operate within a system of limited resources, one that does not and has not consistently embodied the purpose of educating all young people toward success. Extreme structural and systemic obstacles, from school buildings that are literally falling apart to the absence of engaging and relevant curriculum to enormous student caseloads for teachers, all contribute to the rates of schools failing their students.

The problem unique to teaching lies in the "slippery slope" toward resignation—once we concede the demand that every student who enters any school building in this country is supported in reaching their full potential (for the sake of this conversation—high school graduation), the game begins;

politicians, schools, teachers, administrators, and others start to arbitrate who will be served and who will not. It does not take a veteran educator to conclude what the result of such selection looks like.

According to the National Center for Education Statistics (2015), the overall high school graduation rate for students in the United States was 81 percent in 2011–2012, the highest rate since they started tracking graduation rates. However, these graduation rates, predictably, are not consistent for all groups of students. White students graduated at a rate of 85 percent, while Hispanic students were at 73 percent. Black and American Indian students had the lowest graduation rate at 68 percent.

Add to these numbers the fact that, on average, 10 percent of high school dropouts end up incarcerated (that number is an astounding 25 percent for African American dropouts), and we have the formula for the school-to-prison pipeline. Of course, not all students who drop out do so as a result of punitive discipline policies, but these policies and the practices that surround them are a significant factor.

These statistics are important, but they only tell the story from the perspective of 30,000 feet—and we can't really see the young people from up there. This book, in contrast, hopes to bring the focus down to the individual interactions and the individual experiences that contribute to these statistics—with the hope of altering the ways educators, students, communities, and schools interact with each other in order to transform these macrodata toward hope and humanization.

Ultimately, when it comes to schooling, acceptance of any level of failure due to "factors beyond our control" leads to our complicity in the inequities of the system in which we operate: Jason cannot stay in his seat for more than twenty minutes at a time becomes "maybe school just isn't for him"; Veronica enters her class reading far below her grade level—"she is too far behind to even have a chance of success"; Jacob's struggles with English comprehension because he has only been living in the United States for two years becomes "the school can only do so much to support him"; and Brianna's constant defiance of her teachers—"she just doesn't want to learn."

And then we have Franky bringing a knife in his backpack to school—in his mind for his safety and protection. It leads to him being recommended for expulsion. Such filtering out of the "problematic" students who are said to keep others from their learning begins as early as kindergarten and becomes a defining experience for many young people throughout their school years.

Most teachers have no trouble identifying barriers beyond their control that keep young people from learning in their classrooms—and to deny or ignore how heavy a burden they are is unfair to educators taking on this weight. However, what we can and do control has the seeds to change how we respond to those barriers and the system.

When a doctor loses a patient, she mourns that loss of life; when a lawyer loses a case, that defeat resonates and challenges her to do things differently or better next time. However, at most schools when a student drops out or is expelled, frequently we simply go about our business without a word or a question. A relief is felt. The loss of students in urban and high poverty schools has been so normalized that by the time students reach high school, the expectation is to reach June with significantly fewer students than were there at the start in August or September.

And to build a pedagogical foundation on the acceptance that some of our youth are not going to be successful is to accept failure before many of our students even have eyes, hearts, minds, and names. It is to view some young people merely as weeds among gardens of students otherwise ready to learn and grow and blossom as roses. This is the culture we must struggle against in our schools. Restorative justice, including seeking to understand the root causes of student behavior in order to build relational ecologies in our classrooms and schools, though not a panacea, can provide both a set of practices and a paradigm-shifting ideology that can help to cure such normalization of loss in education.

Chapter Four

Preventative Discipline Inside and Outside of the Classroom

"It's the Relationships, Stupid"

Relationships are earned, not given. As renowned progressive educator Herb Kohl (1992) aptly analyzes in his essay "I Won't Learn from You," the reason that many students don't learn what their teachers intend to teach them hour after hour, class after class, year after year is not because they are incapable of learning the material, nor because they don't care about education. Rather, many young people simply choose not to learn *what* is being taught *when* it is being taught from *who* is teaching it to them.

Myriad factors contribute to this active resistance. By the time young people reach ninth grade, most have endured an estimated 11,000 hours of schooling. If they have made it that far, one thing is true: they have learned to adapt to a system that asks them to learn in a very specific way, on a very rigid schedule, and through very limited methods.

For many students this system works. They are able to maneuver through the labyrinth of expectations and, ultimately, feel supported and successful at school. However, for those who do not fit easily into our public education system or who choose to actively fight against it, school treats them, at best, as statistics (50 percent dropout rate in Oakland; 10 percent college going for Latino students; 1 in 3 African American boys suspended; and so on) and, in the worst cases, with impatient disdain and outright aggression.

Only when these young people know and believe that the grown-up in the front of the room truly cares about them, as students, yes, but more importantly as unique individuals, will they open their minds and hearts to learning in the classroom—an environment many consider to be foreign and repressive. As teachers, we are the ones within the institution of schooling, in the most influential position to interrupt the process of disenfranchisement and reconnect students with a sense of educational possibility.

Chapter 2 introduced the concept of preventative discipline to describe the work that is done and the structures that are put in place to meet students where they are at and support them in making choices and taking actions that do not violate a school's expectations and core values. The heart of preventative discipline is relationship building. Without strong and trusting relationships among students, between students and staff, and among educators, community cannot be built, and without a solid community, a restorative discipline model will not be successful.

A TALE OF TWO FRESHMEN: ALEX AND GABRIEL

Alex

Mr. Warren's journey through four years as the history and English teacher for a group of 100 students at East Bay Charter Academy provides an illuminating case study for understanding the importance of relationships in building a foundation of restorative discipline in one's classroom and one's school.

In his third year teaching at East Bay Charter Academy, Mr. Warren developed a new ninth grade critical literacy course. Since he had been at the school for two years, he had established some strong connections with his former students, now sophomores and juniors, and had earned a reputation as a teacher who did not tolerate a refusal to learn in his classroom but who genuinely cared for and supported students. But the new ninth graders did not yet know Mr. Warren, nor had they built an expectation of respect and accountability, and Alex, one of the students in his first period class, made his reluctance clear from the beginning.

Every day, Alex would enter the classroom in his well-worn, black Chuck Taylors and fitted baseball cap turned backward, chatting excitedly with his peers, ignoring Mr. Warren's usual "welcome" or "good morning" at the door. As soon as the class was quiet, focused, and beginning their work, Alex would put his head down on his desk and check out, provoking his teacher to engage him so that he could make a public declaration of how much he did not care about school, learning, or "this class, whatever it's called."

Other days, the disengagement took the form of putting his headphones in at the beginning of class or a well-timed need to sharpen his pencil just as Mr. Warren was starting to give his instructions for the day. Some form of this routine continued on a daily basis for the first few months of school, with Mr. Warren addressing it in different ways, sometimes through confrontation and other times through humor, but always making clear to Alex that he did not have the choice to *not* learn in his class. Mr. Warren knew this was a test, one that he could only pass with persistence, patience, and continued commitment to a student who gave every outward indication that he did not care about his education.

In some ways, managing a classroom of students is like playing a game of poker. As a teacher, you have to pay close attention to everyone and learn to read their signs in order to know how they are going to play. Once you know this, you control the table, knowing when to fold if the time is not right, when to place a modest bet, or when to go all-in in terms of what you ask of students.

By October, a little over a month into the school year, Mr. Warren knew Alex's signs fairly well. Most importantly, he had learned that Alex was extremely intelligent, that he genuinely did want to learn, and that he had an appetite for the attention he received when he correctly answered a question or shared his wide-ranging knowledge on history and politics. Equally as pertinent, Warren had realized that Alex was proud of his identity as a rebel who went against the grain. He had a very sophisticated sense of righteous indignation toward school but he deeply valued education on his own terms.

Herb Kohl (1994) has developed the concept he calls "creative maladjustment" to describe such active refusal on the part of students. According to Kohl, " Creative maladjustment consists of breaking social patterns that are morally reprehensible, taking conscious control of one's place in the environment, and readjusting the world one lives in based on personal integrity and honesty—that is, it consists of learning to survive with minimal moral and personal compromise in a thoroughly compromised world and of not being afraid of planned and willed conflict, if necessary." Alex had learned this concept well.

For the remainder of the semester, Mr. Warren made it a point to engage Alex in ways that validated his subversive identity, sharing readings about historical figures like Emiliano Zapata and Mother Jones with whom he knew his student would identify and crafting questions for class discussion with Alex in mind. Having discovered Alex's love of punk rock music, a passion the teacher shared, Mr. Warren made a list of his favorite political punk rock songs that had shaped his thinking at a younger age.

Though he still maintained his air of detachment, Alex began to engage more and more deeply in class, becoming a leader in many ways. And the morning routine when he entered class turned into a handshake and a warm head nod (and sometimes Alex singing a few lyrics from a Bad Religion or Anti-Flag song from the teacher's list). Mr. Warren was starting to win him over and build a connection of trust and respect with his student.

But at the end of the first semester, Mr. Warren was disappointed to see that, despite his engagement in class and his escalating enthusiasm, Alex was still failing critical literacy, as well as most of his other ninth grade classes.

This dilemma brings forward an important realization about the function of relationship building and restorative discipline practices in schools—to be truly successful they must lead to student achievement.

It is not enough to simply build positive and caring relationships with students if, in the end, they cannot be leveraged to help students succeed. Powerful student-teacher relationships are critical, but they are not the end goal. The theory of action says that if we build relationships of trust, respect, and support with students, they will feel more cared for, confident, and responsible for their learning, and therefore, they will succeed academically. But we must continually check to ensure this is indeed the result.

Mr. Warren felt good about the relationship that was building between him and Alex and how this was shifting his student's presence in class, but the fact that he was still failing was unacceptable. Yet, when he addressed the issue of his grades with Alex, the student reverted back to "I don't care about school" mode. As far as the teacher could tell, Alex genuinely did not care about grades and was unwilling to do the work necessary, work he considered insignificant to and disconnected from his plight to remain independent and true to himself.

Jay Gillen (2014) describes this dynamic succinctly in his book *Educating for Insurgency*. Gillen, a long-time math teacher in the Baltimore public schools, reasons, "Most good teachers of adolescents in schools of poverty feel trapped. We feel unable to meet all the needs of our students, nor can we satisfy the demands of authorities. Most students in these schools feel trapped, too. They spend much of the day doing things they have not freely chosen to do, and endure constant judgment and humiliation as a matter of course" (13).

Within this institution and these feelings of being trapped, educators must fight to build meaningful and humanizing relationships with their students, especially those like Alex, who are most marginalized from feelings of success and belonging in school. This relationship is the starting place for granting their educators the right to demand more of them, to demand that they learn. Ultimately, this is also the foundation for keeping students engaged in behaviors that uphold a school's expectation and core values—and for reengaging them when they take actions that harm themselves and the community. The act of building relationships is a form of preventative discipline.

Given his proclivity for resisting authority, Alex was prone to getting in trouble in school. Singing at the top of his lungs in the hallway, cutting class, refusing to move seats when prompted by a teacher; his transgressions were never seriously harmful to himself or others. Alex's resistance took the form of what is most often labeled "defiance," a catch-all term schools have developed to essentially mean any action a student takes that goes against what a staff member is asking him to do in a given moment.

The fact that these behaviors had ceased in Mr. Warren's classroom, yet they continued in other classes and outside of class, is evidence of the power of relationships. But this did not set the teacher at ease. He knew he had to figure out how to leverage his relationship with Alex not only to turn him into Dr. Jekyll when he walked into critical literacy class, but to eliminate Mr. Hyde altogether. If his same behaviors and levels of engagement in school continued, Alex was on a path toward dropping out. He needed not only Mr. Warren's class but all of his classes in order to graduate. He needed his teachers and administrators to meet him where he was at and help him navigate his way to the commencement stage.

Without the trust and community that comes with relationship building, Alex would never make it through the obstacles and pitfalls that awaited him over the next four years without school being a place where he could fall down, break rules, bang his head against the wall, and know that the adults around him would nurture and support him through the process.

This is why, to be truly successful, it is not enough for one teacher or a single administrator to carry the weight of restorative justice at a school. Alex needed to experience comparable support and care in every interaction with staff at school. Then his choice to learn in that place and time and from that person would be much more compelling. As a school, East Bay Charter Academy needed to construct a network or relationships and support structures that met Alex's creative maladjustment and righteous indignation with an equal amount of care, empathy, and tough love.

Gabriel

Gabriel was another ninth grader in Mr. Warren's critical literacy class. Short, gregarious, and all smiles when he walked through the door, it was obvious from day one that this child was special. And that he was going to be a handful.

Gabriel was deeply engaged in the social aspect of school. He could be the class clown but could also express his knowledge with a combination of intellectual insight, knowledge of self, and worldly awareness rare for any high school student, let alone a young man just beginning his freshman year. Naturally charismatic, he was liked by his teachers and adored by his peers, the kind of student who built bridges and got along with just about everyone. However, by the end of the first few weeks of class, it was apparent he also did not conform easily to the rigid shape of school. He quickly started to fall behind. Although in ways it felt similar to Alex's creative maladjustment, there were more layers surrounding Gabriel's resistance.

The quality of Gabriel's disconnectedness reflected a combination of reluctance and skepticism. It seemed like he was just not convinced that the benefits of school were of great value to him, at least not of enough value to prioritize academic engagement over social fulfillment and attention. Like many students who are unwilling to conform, Gabriel was deeply invested in the aspects of school he valued but resistant to the aspects he deemed unimportant. Gillen (2014) explores this phenomenon in *Educating for Insurgency*;

> Young people evade adult demands not because adults are inexpert in framing those demands, not because adults have yet to find the correct rewards, punishments, resources, environments, and curricula to secure compliance, but rather because the young people have different purposes and different interests from the adults, and are pursuing those purposes and interests according to their own plans, often successfully. (57)

Gabriel was certainly pursuing his own purpose in school, and doing so expertly. But these purposes were not aligned with academic success, even if they did align with his immediate interests and sense of agency. This is one of the paradoxes educators working within schools face—the knowledge that, given the limitations of the society we live in and the function of schools within this society, we must frequently ask students to use their time in ways that do not meet their immediate desires and purposes.

Schools are organized to produce obedient workers (Bowles and Gintis 1976). Although there are innovative efforts to subvert and transcend this structural reality in schools everywhere across the country, educators must still operate within it. They make choices every day and in every interaction that attempt to humanize their students and address their individual needs and dreams. This includes working to convince students like Gabriel that finding a way to play the game in order to be successful in school is for their own benefit.

Gabriel's creative maladjustment, if played out over time, would most likely result in him failing his classes and eventually leaving school. And in a society where nearly one-third of all black male high school dropouts between the ages of twenty and thirty-nine are imprisoned (Coates 2015), this was not a choice his teachers were willing to allow him to make.

Easier said than done. Though Gabriel was a brilliant young man who brought joy to any room he entered, he had also, over the course of nine years and dozens of classrooms, absorbed the narrative that he was simply not a "good student." By the time he entered ninth grade at East Bay Charter Academy, he had stopped trying to pay attention in class when the topic did not interest him, to conform to the will of his teachers and principals, to complete work he found to be irrelevant, and, overall, to be academically successful.

One example that demonstrates Gabriel's dilemma was his experience in geometry. As a freshman, Gabriel tested into tenth grade geometry when over 80 percent of his peers were taking algebra 1. Ms. Loma, his geometry teacher, reflected on how Gabriel would spend his time in class making fun of Euclid or questioning how anyone could care enough about congruent triangles to actually study it in college. When he engaged in class, which was rare, he could pick up on a concept easily. But she could not get him to complete a single assignment.

So Gabriel failed geometry in ninth grade. The same pattern continued in tenth grade—and Gabriel failed again. In the end, Gabriel took geometry for three years in a row before finally deciding to do the work necessary to pass the class. So what did it take to help Gabriel transition to a student who self-identified as a scholar with a sense of purpose that aligned with the demands and requirements of school?

First, it is helpful to refocus the telescope and examine the sophisticated combination of factors, both in school and in his life outside of school, that led him to such a position. The most important thing to know about Gabriel, the factor that stood as the foundation for everything else in his life, was that he was deeply loved and cared for. His family nurtured and cherished him.

During their ninth grade orientation, parents at East Bay Charter Academy were invited to write on an index card a brief note and a goal they wish for their children to accomplish. Gabriel's mother wrote the following:

> Dear Gabriel,
>
> I hope that after you complete high school you continue your education by going to a four-year college of your choice and completing college with the best grades and many carrer [sic] options. I hope you work to obtain the life of your dreams. I love you no matter what.
>
> Son, just don't give up with this education. You can go anywhere and do anything. I believe in you. I love you. God wouldn't put more on you than you can bare. You're a great young Black Man who will move mountains.

Gabriel's family *wanted* the most for him. But his life experience had not set him up for an easy path toward success. A few months into the school year, in his "Testimonio" personal narrative assignment for English class, Gabriel wrote about his family's on-and-off struggles with homelessness. He had spent a significant amount of his childhood without a home. As often is the case with families living in institutional poverty, Gabriel had no relatives who had graduated from college, so he had few models to look to who communicated the purpose and power of academic success as a means of personal and community empowerment.

In many ways, Gabriel was forced to grow up early and be his own example in life. Ms. Loma remembers an incident during her tenth grade family conference with Gabriel's mother. She arrived to their parent-teacher conference reeking of marijuana. While Ms. Loma stepped into her office for a moment to grab some paperwork, she overheard her student scolding his own mom about her showing up high to his conference. "Really mom, really!?" were the only words necessary to demonstrate the complexity of Gabriel's school/life balancing act. Adding to the trauma of his childhood, his older brother had been diagnosed with leukemia when Gabriel was four and a half years old. When Gabriel was only five years old and just beginning school, his older brother died from the disease.

So, by the time he reached ninth grade at East Bay Charter Academy, Gabriel was already carrying the weight of his complicated world on his shoulders, a world that did not always place success in school as the most immediate priority in his life. It was clear that to build a connection with Gabriel and to get him to shift his academic orientation was going to require a serious commitment and persistent work. His teachers and his school had to engage him by convincing him that the adults at the front of the classroom genuinely cared and that school mattered to his life, not just in the future but *right now*.

PROJECT ENGAGE

Enter Project Engage. Project Engage is a targeted mentorship program, founded by a small group of teachers during Gabriel's freshman year, that aims to transform the culture of school by investing in the students who are most at risk of dropping out. The theory of action held by Project Engage is that by hyperinvesting in the most marginalized and vulnerable students, by building deeply trusting relationships inside and outside of the classroom, and by communicating to students an absolute unwillingness to give up on them and their education, teachers can help to heal the broken relationship between these students and school, ultimately leading to individual and community transformation.

In its first year of existence, each of six teachers volunteered to identify five students in whom they wished to hyperinvest in order to build connections that would eventually lead to academic transformation. Participation in Project Engage involved weekly mentoring sessions, consistent lunchtime and after-school tutoring, periodic monitoring of grades and academic progress, and, most importantly, monthly evening or weekend excursions that took students and teachers beyond the walls of the school building.

This last element is critical because meaningful relationships with students, especially those who are most marginalized, are rarely built during a 60-minute class period with thirty young people in the room, two learning targets on the board, desks organized neatly into rows, and standardized tests looming in the background. Furthermore, students who for myriad reasons find school to be an oppressive space construct thick walls to protect themselves from the abuse they experience. These barriers are fortified when they enter into a classroom, and though it is not impossible to get through to them within that space, it is a formidable task.

Gabriel's wall was unusual because it was constructed of laughter and lightheartedness. But it was a wall nonetheless, and any attempts Mr. Warren made to chip away at it in critical literacy class had felt like hitting a rubber mallet against a brick wall. So Gabriel's name was written at the top of his list for Project Engage.

Mr. Warren remembers the initial conversation when he introduced the program to Gabriel one day after class. The student sat opposite his teacher, half attentive and waiting for the conversation to be over so he could go join the hallway tumult. It was not until Mr. Warren started talking about the excursions that Gabriel gave any indication of interest. He would get to go on camping trips, travel to Southern California for a college tour, and maybe even spend several days in Tahoe playing in the snow. Though not excited about the academic elements of Project Engage, Gabriel agreed to give it a try.

Even though he did not know it at the time, this was a transformational moment for Gabriel. Project Engage was a crucial factor in getting him on track and creating a sense of purpose and belonging at school. The program became less important as he grew older because, as he developed a stronger academic identity, Project Engage came to be unnecessary. In fact, by the second half of his junior year, Gabriel had become a Project Engage leader and was mentoring younger students who were just like him in ninth grade.

Project Engage was effective for one reason: relationships. The program leveraged the power of teacher-student relationships to get students to re-invest in their own academic success. And these relationships were built over time by spending time with students outside of the classroom. Teachers took students camping, where they would spend hours reading the stars, telling stories by the campfire, and pushing each other to make it to the top of Eagle Peak after a three-hour hike. Teachers watched alongside their students in a local middle school gymnasium as Nobel Peace Prize winner Rigoberta Menchú Tum discussed the importance of communities working together to create peace. Teachers wandered the campuses of Occidental College, UCLA, and California State University Northridge with their students, who wondered about the im/possibility of seeing themselves there one day.

Ultimately, hours and hours of time together outside of the classroom transformed perspectives in two ways. First, students and teachers saw each other in a new light. Fundamentally, they truly *saw* one another. Students were not simply disengaged youth who did not care about history or algebra, and teachers were not simply aloof authoritarians who understood nothing of the struggles of young people. Their time together was deeply humanizing, helping both groups to see the other as individuals with beliefs, values, characteristics, and identities beyond just their roles as teacher and student.

Second, the Project Engage excursions began to give the students a sense of broader possibility and to see school as less of a barrier and more of a support for that possibility.

Most importantly, the experiences outside of the classroom impacted how students (and teachers) engaged when they walked back into the school building. Gabriel and many students like him needed the Project Engage excursions—and the relationships built through them—to help him see that school did not have to be the enemy, or even an annoyance where he was required to spend nearly half of his waking hours five days per week. He learned trust. He saw that many of the adults in the front of the classroom genuinely cared about him and invested deeply in his well-being and success. And what followed was a belief that school could be a tool that he wielded for his own empowerment. Importantly, Gabriel also realized that he was not required to give up his sense of self in order to achieve success in school. The two were not mutually exclusive, as he had thought coming into ninth grade.

Over time, Gabriel developed the same academic confidence that he maintained in the social realm. He became just as adept at wielding school as a tool for this new purpose as he was at playing the class clown. By his senior year, he was one of the go-to students whenever visitors came to East Bay Charter Academy to learn about the school. With his distinctive humor and charisma, Gabriel would stand in front of rooms full of CEOs, superintendents, local politicians, and fellow students and tell the story of his transformation.

LEARNING PARTNERSHIPS

For both Alex and Gabriel, relationships were the foundation for building what educator Zaretta Hammond (2014) calls "learning partnerships." This concept is important because it brings to light the ultimate purpose of relationship building with students, which is academic success and personal and community empowerment. Meaningful relationships with students can be valuable in their own right.

Students need significant adults in their lives to help them make difficult decisions, to support them through trauma and tragedy, and to hold up a mirror to help them see themselves. Teachers often take on this role. But teachers also hold a unique place in the lives of young people, and if they are not using their influence to guide their students toward academic success, they are being irresponsible. It is one thing to be liked as an educator. That is easy. One simply needs to have minimal expectations and do whatever students ask.

However, to be in a learning partnership with a student is to invest in them so deeply and to build such a level of trust that they give one permission to push her or him beyond what they think they are capable of (Hammond 2014).

Warren remembers distinctly when he first felt this learning partnership start to solidify with Gabriel. It was his tenth grade year and his second year in Project Engage. The group was on their second excursion of the year, a camping trip a few hours north of Oakland—and it turned out Gabriel loved camping. He arrived fully outfitted with camouflage attire, mag light, and a serious sleeping bag he had borrowed from his uncle.

During the trip, teacher and student connected like they were good friends on a weekend backpacking trip in the Sierras. Gabriel taught Mr. Warren what he knew about the constellations as they compared s'mores roasting techniques. Mr. Warren shared with his student accounts of his adventures growing up near the redwoods as they hiked through the very forest that held the stories. On the way home, the two traded DJ responsibilities in the car, the speakers jumping from E40 and Drake to Green Day and Ben Harper, depending on who controlled the dial.

Though the camping trip had been a highlight of the year for Mr. Warren, it was not until the next day at school when he realized the real impact of the weekend. Gabriel walked into second period world history class and greeted his teacher with a warm handshake and a smile. He still did not miss an opportunity to chat it up with his peers and share a few of the jokes he had acquired from the campfire, but when Mr. Warren called him out and asked him to get focused, Gabriel responded immediately by not only quieting down and paying attention himself but also by imploring his classmates to "get focused." When the teacher circled the room to collect homework from the previous class, Gabriel, who almost never completed work outside of the classroom, proudly held his assignment out to be collected. "I got you," he asserted as Mr. Warren gripped the paper.

WE'RE IN THIS TOGETHER

It would be naïve to claim that a camping trip, or any single experience outside of the classroom is a silver bullet that automatically transforms students' orientation to school and sense of academic identity. Developing relationships is much more extensive and complex, as are the factors that lead to young people being marginalized or feeling oppressed by school. But this is also why educators must invest in establishing relationships with their students and why these relationships are a form of preventative discipline and potentially a foundation for restorative justice. When students sincerely believe they are "in it together" with their teachers, they are far more willing to invest in school as a tool for empowerment and transformation.

Chapter Five

When Students Become the Leaders

Letting Go of Punitive Control and Letting Students Lead

Amid the chaos of lunchtime, a lone apple flies across the lunchroom, over tables, through conversations, and slams against the door on the other side of the room. José, the aspiring pitcher, begins to laugh, a satisfied moment of jubilation with two or three friends near him who were in on the scheme. Their laughter quickly fades as the boys realize Ms. Johnson, the principal, has caught them in the act. As she approaches, José turns his back in feigned ignorance. Even though Johnson literally watched as the shiny green apple was released from his hand, José denies throwing it.

At seventeen, José had already experienced enough encounters with authority, in school and beyond, to know that the first response to getting caught must be to deny culpability. Johnson quickly grows frustrated. The confrontation escalates. A few minutes later, José is leaving the principal's office to begin his five-day suspension.

This scenario, repeated in some form thousands of times every day at schools and in classrooms across the country, was the first incident taken on by the newly formed Student Justice Panel (SJP) at The City School (TCS), a small charter school in the San Francisco Bay Area. The SJP was the product of teacher leadership and pressure to move toward a more restorative and responsive approach to student discipline. The initiative had considerable ideological support from several teachers but lacked a clear road map on how to apply this discipline philosophy in the day-to-day life of school.

The City School is a public charter high school serving about 400 students in San Francisco, one of a network of several schools with the mission of: *Transforming the lives of students, especially those who will be the first in their family to attend college, by preparing them for success in college, in careers, and in life.* Students who attend this school reflect the diversity of the city and come from every neighborhood in San Francisco.

The Student Justice Panel is a restorative justice model of school discipline, the purpose of which is to uphold the school's core values and sense of community by working to restore damaged relationships between individuals and the community. The SJP is made up of about twelve student leaders nominated by their teachers and peers; its stated beliefs are that:

- TCS believes strongly in maintaining our Core Values of Discipline, Growth, Community, Justice, and Respect
- Each individual at TCS is responsible for the community as a whole
- TCS functions best when students take leadership and are given a strong voice

SJP hearings consist of an adult facilitator, the community members involved in the violation of the core values, and at least four SJP representatives. Parents or family members may also be present, depending on need. Petitioners and respondents can also request to have additional student advocates present. Everyone at the hearing, including the respondent, will propose consequences aimed at restoration; consequences will be discussed and decided on by the SJP before being implemented.

The shift toward restorative justice at The City School was largely a bottom-up movement. Although administrators were nominally supportive of the push, they were not the engines behind the change. The fuel for the changes came from a few teacher leaders and eventually from students. This continues to be a challenging dynamic at schools that are attempting to implement restorative discipline structure like the SJP, where there never seems to be enough time or resources to do restorative justice right. Furthermore, the relationships and individualized attention needed to properly integrate a restorative discipline model often clashes with the "sacrifice some for the good of the whole" doctrine that drives many school discipline policies.

The City School was by no means a place that relied heavily on punishment and removing "bad students" to maintain its school culture. Every adult in the building genuinely wanted to do what was best for the young people they served. There was, to some extent, already a restorative philosophy at play throughout the school, and a few staff members had attended restorative justice trainings and professional development. However, like many schools with similar missions and goals related to equity, social justice, and college readiness, The City School faced a critical disconnect between what they wanted and what was actually happening as a result of school discipline policies and practices. They wanted to be true to their core values:

Discipline – We discipline ourselves so that no one else has to.

Growth – We are committed to lifelong learning and personal growth.

Community – We work hard and take responsibility for the success of all members of our community.

Justice – We are empowered agents of change for social justice and equity.

Respect – We seek to see the best in each other and treat one another with dignity. We give respect in order to get respect.

They wanted to help students transform mistakes and bad choices into learning experiences. They wanted to create a school culture in which students learned to discipline themselves and each other so that referrals, suspensions, and expulsions would become the exception instead of the rule. But José walking out of the building was an indicator that they were far from reaching these goals. They had so much work to do.

DECIDING TO ACT

When members of the Student Justice Panel learned José had been suspended for five days for what students considered an innocuous act of playfulness, their "justice meters" went into "oh, hell no" mode. After school that day, four SJP leaders rushed into the classroom of Mr. Warren, the teacher who served as the SJP coordinator, filled with urgency and outrage.

"They can't suspend him for five days for throwing an apple," one shouted.

After several minutes of questioning and analyzing the incident and the response to it, Mr. Warren agreed that the SJP had a responsibility to raise its voice and respond to the apple incident.

The SJP students decided that the first step in supporting José was communicating their perspective to principal Johnson. She was reasonable, and she had also shown consistently that she wanted to do right by students.

"Let's go down there right now," one of the students, Nicole, shouted, "I don't care if she is busy; she needs to do something about this!"

Mr. Warren reminded Nicole that Ms. Johnson was not their enemy and that if they approached her as though she was, they wouldn't get anywhere.

"Don't forget Ms. Johnson was actually very supportive of the SJP. We don't want to lose that support by coming at her disrespectfully," the teacher offered his opinion to the group.

"I want to take her to the Student Justice Panel," Nicole exclaimed. "Why does she think she can do this?"

"Petitioning to bring Ms. Johnson to the SJP is actually an option," Mr. Warren replied "but for now let's focus on the situation with Jose and how we are going to get Ms. Johnson to listen to us."

Deondre stepped in. Typically, a quiet and reflective student who kept his thoughts to himself, Deondre was a leader who students trusted to be honest and just. "We need a proposal that makes it clear why we think this is unfair. If we just rush into her office yelling at her, she will never hear us," he said. "And José did throw an apple across the cafeteria. Let's not front like he didn't do anything wrong."

Deondre's reasoning calmed them and sent them into planning mode. They huddled around a desk and started to build their plan. The teacher stepped back and listened, offering a few suggestions, but really just letting them work it out. After about ten minutes, they were excited about their next steps, but they still didn't fully trust that the Student Justice Panel process was real or that Ms. Johnson would listen to them.

Their distrust was not surprising. As discussed in chapter 2, students have become accustomed to the balance of power in schools tipping clearly away from them and toward teachers, administrators, and other adults in the building, regardless of who is standing on the side of what is just.

What makes the SJP so transformative is the shift in the dynamics of power it represents. Many schools have structures that are intended to encourage students to have a voice. But SJP actually has the authority to affect and even change school discipline decisions and policies. At The City School, any community member can bring another member of the community before the SJP for violating any of the school's core values. This can be extremely useful when a teacher is trying to reason with a student who is about to explode because of a perceived unfairness. The teacher can remind the student that she is not powerless in that situation, but that her power does not lie in yelling and demonstrating anger. Her power lies in her peers, who will be the ultimate arbiters of justice through the Student Justice Panel.

The apple incident would be the test to see if the SJP was really functional. Was the school really willing to give students a voice in some discipline decisions and would the principal modify her punishment? Even the teachers who helped form the SJP were initially not certain themselves if the school leadership was willing to give up that kind of power. But they had to find out.

Two of the SJP representatives, who were elected weeks before by peers in their advisory classes, went to Ms. Johnson's office to make an appointment to discuss the incident and their feelings about José's suspension. Ms. Johnson was game. The next day, Ms. Johnson met with the four SJP leaders who initially raised the issue, Mr. Warren, and the assistant principal of school culture.

Equally surprised, nervous, and excited, the four students gathered in Mr. Warren's classroom after school to discuss how to approach the meeting and what to ask for. They decided the fundamental issue was not that José was being punished for his actions but that the punishment did not fit his "crime."

During the conversation, they realized that José held the main responsibility in restoring the situation. They agreed that throwing the apple was wrong and that he needed to have consequences. But a five-day suspension would not accomplish anything except to push him further behind in his schoolwork and make him even angrier about coming to school. Furthermore, using José as an example was unreasonable. The SJP group decided to ask Ms. Johnson to allow José to return to school the next day, having served one day of his suspension, on three conditions. José would be required to:

- write a letter of apology to the janitor (who would have had to clean up his apple mess if Jose had not been caught);
- stay after lunch to clean up the cafeteria for a week; and
- write a reflection about which core values he violated and what it meant to be responsible for his actions at school.

It took less than a half hour to discuss the issue and come up with these consequences. The students walked away feeling good about their proposal.

STUDENTS CHALLENGING INJUSTICE

At the meeting the next day, Deondre, Nicole, and two other Student Justice Panel students presented the proposal to Ms. Johnson, making it clear why they believed their proposed actions were not only more just but actually held José to higher expectations than simply suspending him. Ms. Johnson accepted the proposal. The expressions on the faces of the four students changed as they listened to Ms. Johnson's words. The Student Justice Panel was for real.

José agreed to the conditions and returned to school the next day—anything to avoid the five-day suspension. But, after a few days back, he failed to follow through on one of his commitments—staying after lunch to clean up the cafeteria.

This was a pivotal moment for the nascent SJP. As part of the process of establishing the SJP, those involved had considered what would happen if a student did not follow through with their restorative consequences and decided that this would trigger a return to their punitive consequences.

However, before the situation with José got to this point, students on the SJP—on their own with no adult prompting—spoke with José and convinced him that it was critical for him to keep his end of the agreement, both for his benefit and for the sake of the SJP process. In the following days, José followed through on the rest of his restorative consequences.

This demonstrates one of the powerful unforeseen benefits of the Student Justice Panel: students take leadership and hold each other accountable for discipline. Sure, in this situation, José wanted to avoid more days of suspension. And schools must have discipline policies with punitive consequences to ensure accountability. Students could comply with school policies to avoid being punished for their actions, or students could comply with school policies because their peers hold them to high expectations. When the high expectations approach is at play, students are investing in building and maintaining a positive and respectful school community because they believe they have the voice and the authority to do so.

Apple incidents happen all the time at schools, and it would be naïve and dishonest to say the success of José's case is representative of how the SJP and other restorative structures always work. School discipline is inherently messy and challenging. But if schools genuinely believe their purpose is to serve all students and help them toward paths of success, the Student Justice Panel provides a powerful tool for doing this work.

STUDENT JUSTICE PANEL VERSION 1.0

Schools such as East Bay Charter Academy in Oakland, California, and New Haven Academy in New Haven, Connecticut, took the Student Justice Panel model that was developed at The City School and refined it to function as a more systemic element of their schoolwide discipline policies. While the process is always a work in progress and its efficacy at a school depends on factors such as school leadership, teacher investment, and available resources, the method that has been developed at these schools provides an effective and sustainable model for schools to emulate. This section will provide a general overview of that method and the steps necessary to establish an SJP at one's school.

BUILDING THE FOUNDATION: STAFF BUY-IN

If your school is at the point where you are considering implementing a Student Justice Panel, then you have probably already done some work with students and professional development with staff around the philosophical foundations of restorative justice and you have some restorative discipline structures in place. If you attempt to build an SJP before this work has been done, it will almost inevitably fail. For many teachers, it is an immense shift to go from managing students through a traditional punitive approach to discipline to the restorative orientation of the SJP. For students, trust, agency, and responsibility, qualities that are not fostered by punitive discipline policies, must be built in order to move forward with an SJP.

Once a school has decided to implement a Student Justice Panel, teachers need to be engaged in professional development work around how it will function, including the ways it will potentially impact them. Though the structure functions externally from their classrooms, they may be expected to engage with the process on multiple levels. The most profound shift for teachers and administrators is that the SJP creates an institutional shift in power from the "teacher is always right" framework embodied by traditional punitive discipline.

The SJP gives students a tool to seek redress when they think they have been accused wrongly or treated unfairly by a teacher or administrator. Adults need to be willing to participate in a Student Justice Panel if a student submits a reasonable request, and, ultimately, they must accept consequences suggested by the SJP if it is decided they were in error.

At East Bay Charter Academy, we encountered this situation multiple times. One straightforward example is when Alex, a senior in Mr. Kelley's class (yes, the same Alex from chapter 4) wrote a petition to the SJP saying his math teacher had wrongly accused him of cussing in his class, resulting in a detention.

The panel process revealed that Mr. Kelley had indeed mistakenly accused Alex and he willingly volunteered to revoke the detention and apologize to Alex in front of the class the next day. But the process also gave the teacher a chance to share his perspective, offering that he was having a particularly challenging day with that class and naming how Alex often contributed to an unfocused environment in their math class. Two SJP leaders who were in that same class confirmed Mr. Kelley's claims and Alex was pushed to take responsibility for improving his behavior in the future. In the long run, Mr. Kelley's error and the restorative process that followed resulted in a stronger relationship with his student and a more focused classroom environment.

Consequences for teachers most commonly include simply accepting that one has made a mistake or acted unfairly toward a student, followed by some kind of apology. This is a radical and risky shift for teachers who rely heavily on their positional authority as a source of power in the classroom, and it must be balanced by building a greater sense of responsibility on the part of students. But, in schools and classrooms that have established a strong sense of community, the trust and sense of student agency built overwhelmingly nets a positive impact on classroom management and school culture.

The problem is that it is difficult to believe in or trust the possibility that *giving up* one's authority can actually lead to positive change and increased responsibility on the part of students. You have to experience it to be convinced, and you cannot experience it until the process has been implemented. This is why strong leadership is critical to the establishment of a successful Student Justice Panel. You have to have someone, ideally multiple educators, on staff who have experience with and confidence in restorative discipline practices or expert outside facilitators who can make your staff believe in the possibilities of restorative discipline structures.

Additionally, teachers need to be nurtured and supported through the process of implementation. Feelings of losing control of the classroom or being overwhelmed by the shift are common and must be addressed through clear support structures, coaching, and professional development during the time of transition.

BUILDING THE FOUNDATION: SELECTING AND TRAINING STUDENT REPRESENTATIVES

The most difficult work is changing the hearts and minds of the educators at one's school. Once this has been done, much of the process is technical and involves training student leaders and building awareness of the process among the student body.

One simple and effective way to build trust right at the start is to select Student Justice Panel leaders through a nomination process. At The City School every advisory class nominated one SJP representative so that they were distributed equally across grade levels. Through their advisory class, every student in the school had an SJP representative who also served as a liaison to report back every week with any important messages or actions.

At East Bay Charter Academy, the nomination process turned out to be less systematic. Any teacher, administrator, or student could nominate someone to become a representative, including students nominating themselves. This resulted in a less equal distribution of SJP representatives and a panel that was dominated by eleventh and twelfth grade students, a makeup that had both positive and negative repercussions.

While the lower grades did not have as much voice on the SJP as compared to The City School, East Bay Charter Academy's SJP had stronger leadership due to the maturity of the students. Additionally, because The City School required each advisory class to have an SJP representative, some students became less committed over time because they felt like their involvement was a requirement as opposed to a privilege and a choice. At East Bay Charter Academy, the level of commitment was extremely high because none of the members had joined out of a sense of obligation or peer pressure.

It is important to remember that leadership is a skill. Oftentimes, educators make the mistake of believing student leaders are simply born with the skills and awareness necessary to guide and influence their peers to make better choices and build better schools. But this is rarely the case. So before throwing students into a situation in which they were required to think, communicate, and collaborate on a sophisticated level and to have the courage, moral sensibility, and knowledge of the core values required to hold other members of their community to high expectations, they needed training.

Initially, this orientation involves eight to ten hours of training followed by ongoing reflection and training sessions throughout the year. Students must first be introduced to the philosophical elements of restorative justice, including some examples of how it looks in the world. They then move to the technical and practical aspects of restorative discipline in schools before going over the specific Student Justice Panel process.

Finally, in groups, students work through mock scenarios like the ones they will encounter throughout the school year (see appendix C for a sample SJP training agenda). It is important to note here that in an ideal world, students would undergo significantly more training. However, given the limited resources and time constraints in schools, this level of training is enough to provide students a solid enough foundation to begin the work.

It is crucial for schools who are implementing a Student Justice Panel for the first time to gauge the readiness of SJP leaders before actually implementing this process with real-world situations. At schools where restorative justice is part of the school culture and several other restorative structures are in place, one session might be enough for SJP leaders to be ready for action. At other schools where restorative practices are fairly new, multiple training sessions might be necessary before students feel prepared and confident in holding such an important responsibility. Moving forward too soon with implementation will only make the development of trust and buy-in more difficult in the long run.

BUILDING THE FOUNDATION: PREPARING THE STUDENT BODY

We are almost there. Now that the staff is ready and the Student Justice Panel leaders have been trained, it is time to get the broader student body prepared for the implementation of this new structure, including communicating to them the need to use it responsibly if it is going to be effective.

At East Bay Charter Academy, schoolwide roll out happened through advisory classes. The Student Justice Panel, including their teacher coordinator, created a series of lessons that all advisory classes throughout the school carried out. These lessons followed a journey similar to the SJP member training, though on a much more basic level.

Advisors led their students through an exploration of their beliefs about justice and the ideological differences between restorative and punitive justice, followed by a lesson about restorative justice in the world, using specific historical case studies as examples. Students were then introduced to the specific structures and process of the SJP at East Bay Charter Academy.

Finally, SJP leaders broke into multiple groups and visited each advisory classroom, giving students a chance to offer their feedback, express their concerns, and ask questions to clarify the process.

THE PROCESS

The SJP process begins with a member of the school community (student, teacher, or other administrator) filling out a petition to bring another community member before the panel for violating the school's core values or otherwise causing harm (see appendix B for a sample SJP petition). The petition is turned into an SJP coordinator. This can be a dean, assistant principal, teacher leader, or restorative justice coordinator, depending on the resources a school has available. This person evaluates the petition to assure that it is appropriate for the Student Justice Panel.

Generally, SJP petitions are approved for the panel as long as the petitioner honestly and completely filled out the form and demonstrated how the potential offender violated a core value or harmed another member of the community. In some cases, the SJP coordinator decides that a peer mediation, one-on-one conversation, or restorative circle might be more appropriate.

The petition process is meant to be rigorous enough to ensure students genuinely feel a sense that they or their peers have been wronged before applying for the SJP, but manageable enough as to not overwhelm students. It is important that students take the process seriously.

Once the petition has been approved, a Student Justice Panel is convened. SJP hearings consist of an adult facilitator, the community members involved in the violation of the core values, and at least four SJP representatives. Parents or family members may also be present, depending on need. Petitioners and respondents can also request to have additional student advocates present. Everyone at the hearing, including the respondent, will propose consequences aimed at restoration; consequences will be discussed and decided on by the SJP before being implemented. The following is an outline of a typical SJP hearing:

Opening:

- The facilitator welcomes everyone, reviews the purpose of the SJP, and introduces the community members involved in the hearing.
- The petitioner reads her or his petition letter to the group.
- The respondent offers her or his reactions to the letter and reflects on her or his responsibility in the situation.

Questioning:

- The SJP representatives ask probing questions to determine the level of violation of the core values, what relationships need to be restored, and to fully understand the underlying causes of the situation.
- Petitioner and respondent respond to the questions.

Consequences:

- The respondent first suggests consequences aimed at restoring the community and addressing underlying causes.
- SJP representatives suggest additional or revised consequences, again aimed at restoring the community and addressing underlying causes.
- The respondent leaves the room while the SJP representatives discuss the suggested consequences and decide on which ones will be implemented.
- The facilitator presents the consequences to the respondent, explains the rationale for choosing them, and officially puts them into effect.

Closing:

- The facilitator reviews the consequences to be enforced and the plan of action for holding the respondent and the SJP responsible for implementing them.
- The facilitator assigns one SJP panel member as a liaison to make sure the consequences have been completed.
- The facilitator thanks the SJP for their participation, the respondent for her or his cooperation, and the petitioner for her or his concern and willingness to take action to uphold the core values.

IF YOU BUILD IT THEY WILL COME

Lilia, Khalil, Nancy, and Marcus eagerly entered Mr. Warren's room on the first Thursday that the Student Justice Panel was scheduled to kick off. "Where are we going to meet? How many petitions do we have this week? Do we have enough SJP representatives?" Excitement poured from them.

Mr. Warren, the SJP teacher-coordinator, sat down and announced to the students that no petitions had been submitted for the SJP that week. "But we heard a lot of students talking about it and saying they were going to fill out petitions," responded Lilia. "Are you sure Ms. Brown (the assistant principal of student culture) didn't just lose them?"

"I'm sure. I just checked with her last period, and she said no one had turned in anything to her," the teacher asserted. After a momentary emotional letdown, the students decided that they needed to do more to build awareness and trust around this new discipline structure. They genuinely believe that the Student Justice Panel would give students a voice that they had never had at school before and that it would contribute to a more positive school culture, but not if students did not use it.

After talking to a few of their peers, SJP leaders realized that the main problem was that students did not have a clear sense of how the SJP worked. As Josh, one of the SJP leaders at East Bay Charter Academy, expressed, "A challenge with implementing SJP at East Bay Charter was advertising the availability of it. There would be times when the core values were broken and students would complain instead of taking the situation to SJP. I found it helpful that when situations like this happened, some teachers encouraged students to appeal to SJP; however, not a lot of students naturally resorted to it."

On top of this many doubted that students would really be given power over decisions about discipline. Most just did not have confidence in the process, an understandable stance given their experiences with punitive discipline policies over the past nine, ten, or eleven years. They had to see the SJP working in order to believe it.

SJP leaders decided to reach out to their peers over the next few weeks and push them to utilize the SJP. They were confident that once students actually experienced the process working and saw consequences being given by students and upheld by teachers and administrators, they would start to rely on the SJP more frequently. The buy-in was slow at first, but, over time, it became a structure that students and teachers utilized when they felt like they had exhausted other options or when they felt there was an unfair power dynamic in place.

The next chapter discusses in more detail some of the specific cases that were handled by the Student Justice Panel at East Bay Charter Academy. Due to changes in both teaching staff and administration, the Student Justice Panels at The City School and East Bay Charter Academy have undergone transitions and adjustments over the past several years, at times making progress as important elements in the overall discipline structure of the schools and at other times taking a back seat to other priorities established by the school leadership. To be implemented fully, restorative structures like the Student Justice Panel require the full support of the administration and teachers.

Given the connection between school discipline, dropouts, and the school-to-prison pipeline, the value of such structures is critical. We owe it to José and the myriad students facing similar situations in our schools every day. We need to care deeply enough about his education and his humanity to invest in developing restorative discipline models that thrive in our schools and not simply in systems that punish students when they make poor choices, like throwing apples when the principal is watching.

STUDENT VOICES

In this chapter focused on letting students lead, it feels essential to actually include the voices of students who have served as leaders on Student Justice Panels. Below are excerpts from interviews and surveys conducted with a few of these students.

Cruz

I participated with Student Justice Panel at EA because I was a part of the Student Leadership Group. I joined the Student Leadership Group because I wanted to be more involved with my school and develop my leadership skills. The Student Justice Panel was really interesting because, with the situations being presented, I felt like I became able to look at things dichotomously. A skill like that has been truly helpful in my first year in college.

The purpose of Student Justice Panel is to remedy tensions between parties. SJP is unique because it allows both parties of a situation to move on from a certain incident by coming up with specific plans to make sure core values are not broken again. This way, relationships are not ended bitterly but actually strengthened. I believe that the SJP helps strengthen the staff-student relationship by allowing students to remind staff that they can make mistakes too. With the student-to-student interpersonal relationship, I believe that the SJP allows students to handle issues in a more adult manner, and this skill will definitely be helpful in college and beyond.

Students are definitely given a voice with SJP. There was this one incident where one of my classmates was given a detention because the teacher thought that he cursed in class. He took the incident to SJP, and he was able to mitigate the situation that he had with the teacher, had the detention removed, and improved their relationship.

The Student Justice Panel makes school culture at EA a unique one and sets EA apart from other schools. The SJP makes EA more of a community-based school and makes the small-knit campus even more small-knit. The SJP creates a school culture where students can advocate for themselves when a wrongdoing has been committed and create change when change is needed.

The SJP strengthens the core values significantly. Community and growth are strengthened because, by going to SJP, the parties involved are given the chance to express their thoughts of disapproval for someone's actions, fix relationships, and learn how to settle disputes in a mature way.

I think SJP could be made stronger by having the ideas of restorative justice taught in class. Maybe if restorative justice became some sort of unit in an advisory class, the SJP could be promoted and students might be more interested in taking advantage of the SJP when they find it necessary.

Alba

My experience in participating in the Student Justice Panel was an amazing experience, an experience where students can have their voices heard within the community of my school. How I would describe the purpose of the SJP is to build a healthy and a just community. Usually when a teacher gives a punishment to a student, the student is most likely going to react in a nega-tive way. They assume that their punishment is "unfair." But when a member of the SJP gives the punishment, the student is most likely to listen and accept their consequences. What it is intended to do at EA is to bring fairness and justice to the students that allows everybody to learn in a safe environment.

My participation in the SJP impacted me as a student and as a leader because it has made me more open-minded, knowing there are always going to be two sides of a story and knowing how to actually think critically and how there can be more options available to bring justice to the school and to the students. Being part of the SJP has given me ideas on what I want to do with my career. I want to do so many things, but part of what I want to do with my life is to help bring justice to poor communities. I'm thankful that the SJP community gave me this kind of exposure because, as a freshman in college, I am actually struggling with what I want to do as my future career.

Lilia

The most important thing about the SJP is that it gives voice to the students to let them defend themselves. I remember when it was Alex and Mr. Kelley (the incident discussed above). Mr. Kelley took fault for how he falsely ac-cused a student just because he was frustrated. That feels good. Mr. Kelley admitting he was wrong allowed Alex to take responsibility for when he actually did do something wrong.

Usually students go back and forth with the teachers trying to prove themselves right but they usually do it aggressively. But then they just get shut down or sent out. Instead, with the SJP they can keep their cool in the moment and later on bring it up in a more professional way. They know they will be heard.

Being a part of Alex's Student Justice Panel was a powerful experience for me. The guy who "knows everything" and who pretends that he doesn't really care, him going and defending himself, showed me how serious or dedicated he really was about his education. This changed my perception of him.

Khalil

Typically, institutions tend to have predetermined consequences for certain situations. For example, in schools it can vary from things like the detention system to the process of suspension and/or expulsion of a student. With this in mind, schools tend to resort to them as the only options to address issues that may present themselves. However, the Student Justice Panel allows for there to be, as is said in the name, a more just solution.

One of the reasons that I decided to get involved with the SJP is because it allows students to have a voice within their school community. Usually, students have little to no voice when it comes to addressing certain issues within their school, and many things go unspoken about because there is no opportunity for them to be challenged. And that is what the SJP provides. Opportunity. It gives students the chance to change something if they think it's wrong. It allows them to challenge a grade they believe is deficient, provide an alternate consequence for one they think is too severe, or repair a relationship with somebody before it becomes unhealthy. But most importantly, it provides them with the confidence to be able to speak up for themselves, something they probably wouldn't do otherwise.

One of the things that I enjoyed about participating in the SJP was its flexibility. The range of topics that can be brought up are infinite. The stereotype is that the SJP is only for addressing discipline issues, but that is not the case.

Another reason [the SJP is important] is because the people who can sit on the panel range from students to teachers, to staff, and even community members. The diversity of the panel allows for there to be less bias for any solution that is brought forth. This is because the panel members may not know the person beforehand, and/or because it will not just be adult staff handling the case, as typically done in the absence of the SJP.

Chapter Six

Restorative Justice as Twenty-first-Century Leadership Skills

Thinking Critically in a World of Social Disorder

Think Critically. Collaborate Productively. Communicate Powerfully. The current educational trend is pushing many schools to adopt some version of these twenty-first-century leadership skills, and more and more, schools are being structured to help students develop these skills. They go by different names, but they serve the same purpose—provide students a framework for what schools, informed by the professional working world, believe it takes to be a productive member of society in the twenty-first century.

The tendency by some is to view these skills purely in the academic or intellectual realm; work that is done in the head; work that can be assessed through multiple choice testing or other quantitative assessments; work that happens in math, science, history, or English class. However, to unlock the full potential of these leadership skills, we must practice and build them with students in more complex ways, including their social and emotional aspects, as elements to be developed.

Herein lies a convincing opportunity for the role of restorative discipline in schools. As Thorsborne and Blood (2013) assert, "Working restoratively and relationally helps to build classrooms where all students are recognized and valued, where there is high support and high expectations, where these are clear and students learn to self-regulate and assist in regulating the behavior of their peers" (51).

Given the innumerable demands placed on schools, school leaders, and teachers, and the constant struggle to maximize learning within the limitations of class time, instructional minutes, and the test-driven milieu pushed

67

by fixed core standards, building learning opportunities by giving students voice and responsibility in the realm of school discipline and, specifically, through restorative discipline structures is a win-win situation.

While responding to student behavioral transgressions inevitably requires class time and school resources, benefits—academic, social, and emotional—emerge if we authentically engage students in the discipline process. Moreover, one fundamental outcome of restorative justice discipline practices is to keep students in school and in the classroom whenever possible, resulting in improved academic performance.

However, too frequently when it comes to issues of behavior and school discipline, students are forced to put these skills on hold and just obey, trusting in the unquestioned rightness of the adult who is asking them to behave, or not behave, in a certain way.

Teacher Jay Gillen (2014) elucidates this dynamic in his book *Educating for Insurgency,* "The young are rarely interpreted as fully human actors. More frequently, young people are observed and analyzed as part of the scenic background for the authorities' actions, as props or mannequins, objects upon which older people deploy their stimuli to produce the 'mandated' responses" (50).

Schools and teachers tend to champion critical, independent thinking, powerful communication, collaboration, and other essential skills of leadership when they are wielded in a way that fits within the guarded structure they have established or when they can be in control. For example, teachers love it when students work together in their groups to discuss and make meaning of a challenging reading, but most are not enthusiastic when those same students organize to push back against an assignment they collectively believe to be unfair. And administrators laud student ambassadors who show adult visitors around their school, sharing their stories of how their school has helped them transform their lives, but they discourage students from critiquing the ways the school might be co-opting their stories in order to create a school image that may not be entirely true.

But, when that leadership becomes uncomfortably independent or even insurgent, there is an institutional response to quell that energy and create conformity. The message students receive, both explicitly and implicitly, is that there is a time and a place to exercise leadership skills.

Gillen (2014) further explores this paradox, "Young people know intuitively that they must figure out how to become adults, but that their schools are designed to infantilize them, to simplify and standardize their verbal expression, to restrict and control their bodies, to crush independent, nonconforming thought" (63). The traditional "teacher is always right" paradigm of school discipline, upon which most schools are still founded today, does not allow room for the very twenty-first-century leadership skill development that these same schools hold up as the ultimate goal of education in contemporary society.

This paradox illuminates a critical missed opportunity—one that could fundamentally change the nature of discipline in schools while teaching students to resolve conflict, to think critically, to collaborate, to communicate powerfully, and to carry these leadership skills beyond the walls of one's school as leaders in an imperfectly democratic society. University of Toronto Professor Kathy Bickmore (2005), in her article "Incorporating Peace-Building Citizenship Dialogue in Classroom Curricula" reasons, "When students have opportunities to participate in inclusive, well-facilitated dialogue for restorative justice and interpersonal conflict resolution (instead of punitive discipline), they often develop democratically relevant skills, dispositions, and relationships that can help them address future conflicts peacefully and fairly" (18).

THE POWER OF AGENCY

The pivotal shift from punitive to restorative response centers around the level of agency given to students in the discipline process and the security of school staff to trust students and this system. Punitive school discipline models position students as completely passive actors in incidents of behavioral transgression. For perpetrators, victims, and involved community members alike, they are objects being acted upon by a dean, a principal, a teacher, or a school policy that holds unmitigated power. Under this paradigm, student agency is negligible because consequences or punishments have been decided before the transgression has occurred.

Furthermore, the nature and severity of the punishment is guided by an often-arbitrary set of rules and guidelines that may have no relevance to the offending behavior. Coming drunk to school might carry a three-day suspension, while carrying a pipe with marijuana residue results in a five-day exclusion. Cussing at a teacher leads to a five-day suspension, while using hateful language toward a peer merits only a referral to the dean. These punishments are not universal, and they vary from school to school, district to district, and state to state—a fact that demonstrates the arbitrariness of such standard punitive measures.

Additionally, most schools employ some kind of progressive or escalating discipline policy so that each offense, regardless of the nature of the offending behavior, brings with it a more serious punishment. Progressive discipline policies are akin to three-strikes laws adopted in California and other states. So, for example, at East Bay Charter Academy if a student received her third behavioral referral, regardless of the offense, the policy required that she be suspended for a full school day. It did not matter if the transgression involved a verbal altercation, defiance, skipping detention, or, paradoxically, cutting class. If it was the third offense, the student was suspended for a day.

Of course, depending on the offense, the punishment could be more severe—but according to the policy it could never be *less* severe. The subjective nature of such rigid punitive policies harms students both because the consequence rarely matches the offending behavior, nor is it intended to do so, and, as I mentioned above, it removes students from any meaningful participation in the discipline process. Lesson learned: when it comes to matters of student discipline, critical thinking, collaboration, and powerful communication may not apply.

Agency, in sociological terms, is the ability for people to make independent choices in a given situation and to act on their choices. Fixed punitive discipline structures and policies allow students minimal agency. Once students have made a choice or taken action that has broken a school rule, policy, or expectation, they may be stripped of options, as well as the ability to respond meaningfully and responsibly to their transgression. Even if they realize their error (which they often do) and they wish to involve themselves in repairing and making amends for their actions, this possibility is removed in favor of a preestablished consequence. It also denies them a real opportunity to learn about their own behaviors, responsibilities, and sense of feeling fairly or kindly treated. Additionally, other community members who may have been involved in or impacted by the incident are also excluded from the process.

Restorative justice, however, intentionally places the offender, as well as other involved community members, at the center of the discipline process, not only allowing but insisting upon a high level of agency. Everyone involved is required to play a role in finding appropriate solutions and restoring any harm that was done.

Renjitham Alfred has been a trailblazer and an innovator in implementing restorative justice practices in schools. In her report that was written in collaboration with Jon Kidde, "Restorative Justice: A Working Guide for Schools" (2011), they make clear "the structure [of restorative justice] is different from what we have learned to expect from our systems. Restorative Justice encourages us to be constantly present, attending to needs as they arise. It exercises our ability to be dynamic rather than static in our responses" (5). Placing young people in dynamic situations, involving multiple interests and without a simple solution, is a catalyst for the development of critical thinking, collaboration, and communication skills.

In a way, engaging students in the restorative discipline process is a form of project-based learning where the school incident provides the text for their learning. The dynamic nature of the approach puts young people in positions where they are required to assess an incident that broke school rules, expectations, or core values, reflect on the role they played in the incident, evaluate the best way to respond, restore, move forward, and, finally, to take action based on their evaluation—the essential elements of critical thinking.

CRITICAL THINKING

Critical thinking is a term that, due to the pervasiveness of its use, can mean many things or nothing at all. It is perhaps the term used most frequently to define the goal of schooling, but it is also a term that is rarely given specific form and content. People, educators and non-educators alike, just know that we need to get our young people to *think*.

The definition we will use for this text comes from a statement by Michael Scriven and Richard Paul, presented at the 8th Annual International Conference on Critical Thinking and Education Reform (1987): "Critical thinking is the intellectually disciplined process of actively and skillfully conceptualizing, applying, analyzing, synthesizing, and/or evaluating information gathered from, or generated by, observation, experience, reflection, reasoning, or communication, as a guide to belief and action" ("Defining Critical Thinking," 2013).

This definition is quite broad, but it is useful in helping us conceptualize restorative discipline as a tool for critical thinking in schools for two main reasons: 1. it maintains that information is gathered or generated from multiple sources, namely "observation, experience, reflection, reasoning, or communication"; and 2. it affirms the need for thinking to guide beliefs and actions. So how do restorative justice processes in schools build critical thinking skills? Let's start with the idea that thinking is best forged in the fire.

Most conflicts in schools arise due to feelings. Students get into conflicts, both verbal and physical, when emotions are heightened. Teachers and students scream at or disrespect one another when they get angry or frustrated. Administrators overreact when they are feeling overwhelmed or disregarded. One step in the restorative process is to get participants to step back and think through their actions and their involvement in an incident that harmed the community. This might be as simple as asking a student to step outside to fill out a reflection form (see appendix D for an example) before a friction escalates to full-on conflict in the classroom, or as complex as a healing circle involving fifteen community members. Regardless of the seriousness of the incident, the need for critical thinking is crucial in order to move to a better place and a safer classroom—one that is more enhanced for real learning.

It is important to note here that the restorative justice process is not intended to eliminate emotions as part of the process of moving toward resolution. Humans are emotional and relational beings. To ask people to avoid *feeling* in a given situation is a form of dehumanization, a dynamic that is exacerbated when we bring in racial, gender, class, language, or other power dynamics that are often present in schools. As discussed in chapter 2, emotions can evolve into negative and explosive actions when they are not understood, respected, and treated with care. Righteous indignation becomes rebellious behavior when students are not given an outlet to express, reflect on, and work through their reasonable and justified sense of anger, frustration, or resentment.

But bringing in the head allows us to balance the fire of the heart in order to move forward in a humanizing, respectful, and accountable way. If anything, the reflective and analytical components of the restorative discipline process help all individuals involved to understand the source of others' emotions, as well as their own role in the incident.

SHIFTING PERSPECTIVES THROUGH A STUDENT JUSTICE PANEL

Let's look at the example of Darlene, who was an eleventh grader in Mr. Logan's Algebra II class. She was an excellent student who prided herself on her academic accomplishments. So when her math teacher accused her of cheating on a unit test and assigned her a "0" for her grade, she was incensed. Mr. Logan, usually very even-keeled and understanding, shut down when Darlene came at him ready to go to battle. The two quickly drew their lines on the classroom tile and refused to budge. After multiple failed attempts to be heard by the other, they finally decided to bring the issue to the Student Justice Panel.

The Student Justice Panel, as discussed in the previous chapter, is a restorative justice structure that places students in charge of handling the response to specified discipline issues and seeks to find creative solutions to incidents that have harmed the community. By placing their conflict in the hands of the Student Justice Panel, Darlene and Mr. Logan knew they were giving up their autonomy in resolving the issue, a risk for both but especially for the teacher, who held the formal power in the situation.

For Mr. Logan, referring the matter to the Student Justice Panel required a high level of trust in the process, as well as a recognition that his take on the cheating incident may have been imperfect and, therefore, acting in isolation had its problems and limitations. This decision to stand on equal ground with Darlene in a situation that typically assumes the teacher is always right is one that would make many teachers uncomfortable.

One of the significant challenges of implementing a restorative discipline program in schools is the hesitation on the part of teachers and staff to give equal voice and authority to students when disagreements arise. However, in taking equal responsibility for correcting harm done, Mr. Logan's actions communicated to his student that he valued her perspective, but that it also required her to assume the same level of responsibility. She could no longer regard the incident simply as a rash decision made by a mean or unfair teacher acting unilaterally based on false assumptions.

One of the innate benefits of a commitment to the restorative discipline process is that by modeling accountability to one's own behaviors and actions, others are compelled to hold themselves accountable in different ways. By placing himself on equal footing with his student, Mr. Logan had already shifted the nature of the conflict and shown Darlene that his goal was to resolve it in a fair way, not simply to punish her or assert power over her.

After hearing from both Darlene and Mr. Logan about the cheating accusation, the Student Justice Panel concluded that the student did, indeed, demonstrate poor judgment but that her actions did not constitute cheating as she conceived it. Although she did not actively supply answers for the peer whose test mirrored her own, she could have done more to ensure that her test was not being copied. They also agreed that Mr. Logan was in the wrong when he called out Darlene for cheating in front of the entire classes, the act about which she was most concerned in the first place because she valued her academic identity.

Both teacher and student held some responsibility in the situation and both would share in the consequences. Mr. Logan would offer an apology to Darlene in front of their class and explain why he had assumed she was cheating. He would also create a new "testing" seating arrangement that made it more difficult for students to see each other's papers. Darlene was required to hold afterschool tutoring sessions with the student who had copied from her test, after which both students would retake the test for a new grade. She would also offer an apology to Mr. Logan in front of their class for raising her voice and talking to him disrespectfully when he accused her of cheating.

Both petitioners walked away feeling like they had "won" and, as is most often, though not always, the case with the Student Justice Panel, the outcome was a positive one. However, the true power of the Student Justice Panel, as in all restorative discipline structures, lies not in the outcome but in the process, a process that cannot transpire without rigorous critical thinking from all parties.

Josh, one of the Student Justice Panel leaders, explains, "I think SJP really helped with thinking critically. With SJP, you learn how to listen, analyze, and think about ways in order to mitigate a situation. I found this helpful when it came to my College Success Portfolio (a final academic portfolio required for graduation) because instead of listening to other people's accounts on a situation, I was listening to questions from my panel and thinking about what to answer."

Students on the panel are required to listen as objectively as possible to multiple accounts of a given situation, then to process and analyze the evidence together in order to respond appropriately to the incident. In the case of Darlene and Mr. Logan, they had to place themselves in the shoes of both teacher and student to understand how each felt in that moment and why they had acted as they did.

Luz, a student leader who participated in Darlene and Mr. Logan's panel, describes her thinking, "Being on the SJP you have to throw away your bias about certain people to let them actually defend themselves and have a chance at justice. Usually when the panel spoke to each other once the [petitioner and respondent] were outside, there were almost always a couple of students that defended and some students who spoke against the petitioner so that we could really hear every perspective."

Then, once the panel has come to a conclusion on the levels of fault and responsibility, they must agree upon meaningful consequences. This requires another layer of thinking and creativity, as they push beyond the traditional punitive repercussions available at most schools to find consequences that hold all people involved appropriately accountable.

Everyone involved in the SJP process is asked to listen openly to multiple perspectives, to analyze, and to reflect. Then, as a group, SJP leaders are asked to synthesize and evaluate the evidence and to make a decision. Furthermore, all of these skills are being used in an authentic situation that has an immediate impact on individuals in their school community. In terms of developing a learning experience that exercises critical thinking, it would be difficult to generate a lesson in the classroom that has as much bang for the buck as the Student Justice Panel.

THE PROCESS: THINK, COLLABORATE, COMMUNICATE

Student Justice Panel

As the anecdote above demonstrates, the Student Justice Panel process requires all participants to work together to resolve conflict in a way that holds them appropriately accountable while at the same time building and rebuilding a sense of community and well-being. This begins with a written reflective process that asks the petitioner (the community member requesting to bring her or his peer before the Student Justice Panel) to understand why they are requesting a panel in the first place. They must think through which core values or school expectations were violated, how the broader community may have been impacted, and what role they played in the incident, including what actions they did or did not take to address the issue before bringing it to the Student Justice Panel.

Given the incident, this might be straightforward, if, for example, the harm involves one student clearly insulting another student. However, violations of core values in schools are rarely black and white. Take the cheating incident described above. Darlene's description of what happened differed significantly from Mr. Logan's perspective, and through the petition process, the two were asked to consider not only what was done *to* them but what role they played in the incident and what, if anything, they could have done differently.

Another memorable example that demonstrates the power of this reflective process involved a student at East Bay Charter Academy petitioning to bring another student to the Student Justice Panel for constantly disrupting her learning. This student maintained that her peer was violating the core values of growth, discipline, and community in multiple classes they shared because he was always disruptive and distracting in class, leading to a loss of learning time. The reflective process built into the Student Justice Panel petition, even before it went through the full panel, insisted on critical thinking in multiple ways.

First, the student petitioner had to move beyond her role as passive observer in the class and ask herself if she could have done anything differently to address the troubling behavior. To be clear, it would be unfair and unrealistic to place the burden of classroom management on any individual student in the classroom. Still, while it is the responsibility of the teacher to establish and maintain a focused learning environment, for myriad reasons, this does not always happen, and it can be transformative to push students to understand themselves as active agents within the classroom.

So the student petitioner had to consider the role she played in that community of learners. Second, the student who was accused of violating the core values was forced to step into the shoes of other students, particularly those who had a different relationship to the classroom than he did. Through this he realized that his antics were not viewed by all of his peers simply as fun and games to pass the time and get other students to laugh. Many students were genuinely interested in learning what the teachers were trying to teach and felt annoyed and frustrated by his diversions. Just as in the case of Mr. Logan accusing Darlene of cheating, the preliminary preparation for the Student Justice Panel shifted the nature of the conversation and brought the students together in a more open and accountable way than a traditional punitive approach would have.

Once the actual Student Justice Panel procedure begins, the level of intellectual rigor increases and broadens to include the leadership skills of collaboration and powerful communication. At this point, the panel also engages a new group of participants who were not actors in the original incident but who, as members of the community who have received some training in restorative justice, have volunteered to hold the space and take responsibility for helping their peers to make amends and reach a resolution that feels fair and just to all. The panel ends with the group agreeing through consensus to the resolution and consequences, which are written up and signed by all participants.

The interplay of the core twenty-first-century leadership skills during a well-facilitated panel process is powerful. Both the petitioner and the offender, as well as any additional participants who have come to speak on their behalves, are challenged to think critically and communicate powerfully as they formulate their positions and try to help the panel understand why they chose to participate in a certain behavior or how it impacted them. Through a series of questions, the participants are pushed to provide specific examples and evidence that demonstrates the thinking behind their choices.

Oftentimes, the question-and-answer process is the place where students experience the "aha" moment that shifts their understanding of the incident and allows them to move forward in a different way. For example, in Mr. Logan and Darlene's Student Justice Panel, the question was posed to Darlene, "Why would Mr. Logan want to accuse you of cheating if he did not actually think you did it? How does he benefit from this?"

This gave the student pause and she responded honestly, "This is the first time I have felt like Mr. Logan has done something like this. He knows I am a good student and I think he does want me to do well in his class." This exchange was followed by a series of questions that helped move Darlene from her "teacher-as-villain" stance to a more nuanced position that allowed her to see her teacher as a well-meaning individual who had acted in the moment based on the evidence he had in front of him.

She firmly maintained that he was mistaken in accusing her of cheating but she opened up to understanding how he could have perceived the situation in this way. Similarly, when Mr. Logan was faced with the question of whether or not Darlene had ever cheated or been dishonest before, he was pushed to rethink his hastily drawn conclusion that she clearly knew what she was doing and chose to cheat despite knowing it was wrong. In that moment, he had a revelation that would change his teaching for as long as he stayed in the classroom. Strategic questions from the panel moved both teacher and students to assess the situation differently.

Ultimately, in framing an incident as a text to be interrogated deeply and understood with clarity, albeit a text to which the participants have very real and emotional connections, all parties involved are able to learn from mistakes and transgressions while at the same time shifting their thinking and, ideally, their approaches to similar situations in the future.

Participating in the Student Justice Panel requires students to collaborate as they discuss, debate, and decide on the most meaningful and appropriate consequences for the incident brought before them. Additionally, as exemplified in the situation with José in chapter 5, SJP members must work together to assure that offenders understand and follow through with their assigned consequences.

After all participants have been given a chance to speak their truths and take responsibility for their roles in a given incident, the panel is charged with deciding on an appropriate response, one that matches the harm done or the core value broken and, ideally, leaves the community more connected than it was before. This is often a very challenging step for several reasons, including:

1. limited resources at a school's disposal;
2. the need to build in follow-up that does not place too much burden on teachers and staff who are already overwhelmed with responsibilities beyond the classroom; and
3. limitations of nonpunitive structures and tools in place in a school's discipline system.

Due to these factors, collaborating to decide on consequences is a creative process, requiring Student Justice Panelists to work beyond, around, and through existing structures to find consequences that truly fit the criteria of being restorative, fair, and transformative.

Ultimately, it is not always possible to identify consequences that fit all of these criteria, so the job of the panel is to get as close as they can while maintaining the integrity of the restorative process as much as possible. In a way, the need to be creative and to work within a broader educational discipline system that frequently does not align with the values of restorative justice is a stimulus for the kind of thinking, communication, and collaboration advocated by the framers of the twenty-first-century leadership skills. Students are placed in real-world situations with no predetermined solutions but whose outcomes genuinely matter. Then, given a set of core values and restorative justice principles, they must work together to find a way forward.

In an institution where relevant and meaningful learning experiences can be hard to find and where we work incredibly hard to simulate experiences that ask students to think critically, collaborate, or communicate powerfully, the Student Justice Panel provides an authentic context where these leadership skills can be practiced and honed.

Circles

Circles, probably the most common restorative justice structure used in the school setting, also engage students in the authentic and meaningful use of the twenty-first-century leadership skills outlined above. While there are many different kinds of restorative circles used for various purposes, this section will speak about them in general terms in the context of how they exercise these leadership skills.

Longtime restorative justice practitioner Renjitham Alfred and coauthor Jon Kidde (2011) explain that the purpose of circles is "to bring people together in a way that gives voice to every individual. . . . It is an egalitarian method of communication that can be used to celebrate successes, discuss challenging topics, make decisions, or address wrongdoing" (15). By their very nature, restorative circles develop the skill of powerful and honest communication. Community members are required to speak honestly and openly while holding the integrity of the circle until all participants have had a chance to speak. This might involve a single round of speaking or multiple rounds, depending on the nature of the incident being addressed.

At Rise Up High School, a small public charter school in Oakland's Fruitvale district, all students begin their week with a talking circle in their advisory classes. Every Monday, students rearrange the desks into a circle as they enter advisory class. Once students are seated so that they can all see each other, the teacher offers a prompt to begin the conversation.

Prompts range from a specific topic relevant to social, political, or cultural events to general questions such as "How was your winter break?" Students are encouraged but not required to speak, and the depth of the talk ebbs and flows, depending on the prompt, the mood of the class, and the moments when individuals choose to go deep with their sharing.

These moments are when the power of talking circles can be seen, when students find their words and trust their voice enough to speak what is truly on their minds and in their hearts. They are called upon to give words to their ideas and experiences. At times talking circles flow into more Socratic dialogues, during which students defend, debate, and analyze their own ideas and the ideas of their peers.

The goal of talking circles at Rise Up is to build community and help students and teachers see, know, and understand each other as the year goes on. However, the outcomes reach beyond this goal, empowering students as more confident and eloquent communicators, as well as building a foundation of trust and respect for when more challenging conversations or conflicts emerge in the community.

TWENTY-FIRST-CENTURY LEADERSHIP SKILLS: EDUCATING FOR GLOBAL CITIZENSHIP

If schools are truly going to educate young people to become leaders in the twenty-first century, then they need to create spaces inside and outside the classroom for critical thinking, collaboration, and powerful communication to flourish. As Bickmore (2005) asserts "Given existing, imperfectly-democratic societies, interrupting the status quo—by inviting problem-posing, praxis, and critical dialogue about conflicts—is essential to living democracy, and to build sustainable peace" (18).

When it comes to leadership development, most schools today operate like overprotective parents who, out of fear and distrust, hover over their children and refuse to remove the training wheels as they hobble along the sidewalk nearly tipping over with every pedal. Students are given highly structured and highly limited opportunities to exercise their leadership skills in real-world scenarios that involve actual risk and meaningful outcomes. Of course, they will occasionally make mistakes and they will certainly fall down, but giving young people voice, agency, and authority through structures like the Student Justice Panel and restorative circles provides critical preparation for the challenges of citizenship and leadership that lie ahead.

Academic Impact of Restorative Justice in Schools

While direct links between restorative discipline and academic performance are difficult to measure, an increasing body of research suggests that restorative discipline practices and policies in schools do improve academic success in concrete ways. Oakland, one of several major urban school districts in the United States transitioning toward restorative justice as the foundation for discipline in their schools, provides an illustrative example of the impact of such programs. The Oakland Unified School District has undergone a ten-year process of transitioning toward restorative justice. In a report released in September 2014 entitled, "Restorative Justice in Oakland Schools Implementation and Impacts," produced for the US Department of Education Office of Civil Rights, the following data on academic outcomes are detailed (Jain, Bassey, Brown, and Kalra, vi):

- Twenty-four percent drop in chronic absenteeism in RJ schools, compared to a 62.3 percent increase for non-RJ schools
- Reading levels as measured by SRI in grade 9 increased 128 percent in RJ high schools, from an average of 14 percent to 33 percent, compared to an increase of only 11 percent in non-RJ schools
- From 2010 to 2013, RJ high schools experienced a 56 percent decline in dropout rates in comparison to 17 percent for non-RJ high schools

- Four-year graduation rates in RJ schools increased significantly more than non-RJ schools in the past three years post-RJ intervention—a cumulative increase of 60 percent for RJ schools, compared to 7 percent for non-RJ schools

Chapter Seven

Starting Young

Restorative Justice Discipline Practices at the Elementary School Level

With Contributions by Jeremiah Jeffries

ON SCHOOL CULTURE

In moving toward a school culture that is restorative, elementary, middle, and high school communities require different arcs of implementation, although the desired outcomes for students and staff are the same. At the middle and high school levels, there are many more relationships for adults and youth to negotiate and less time to do so during the school day. Additionally, constant transitions between classes and spaces, unsupervised by adults, create more opportunities for conflict.

Elementary schools differ from middle and high schools most significantly in the volume of students a teacher must interact with and have capacity for, as well as the time available to build relationships with students. In elementary schools, teachers have anywhere from 18–35 students in their classrooms and students spend almost the entire day (four to six hours) with that one teacher. Conversely, at the middle and high school levels teachers must negotiate relationships with 60–200 students and only have 45–90 minutes per day together.

Given this structural reality, at the elementary level, one teacher can have a near complete overview of the relationships between the students and know the impact of their decisions and actions on the climate of the classroom and the school. This also means that a single classroom climate can define or dominate a student's entire experience of school for that year.

In elementary schools, a student can be more easily isolated and protected from the elements of a school's larger culture. There can also be significantly less reliance on the structures and systems outside of the classroom, if the teacher has established a healthy climate and a restorative culture within the classroom.

In the elementary classroom, restorative practices are almost indistinguishable from good teaching. In this chapter, we will look at: 1. foundational elements of restorative discipline practices in elementary classrooms; and 2. a youth leadership model being used to address school climate when conflict arises.

One thing to keep in mind is that for restorative practices to be successful in any context, they must take place within the context of a restorative culture and there must first be relationships to restore. How do teachers establish and maintain positive and powerful relationships to create a prosocial classroom culture before conflict arises?

FROM STRANGER TO SCHOLAR TO TEACHER

In the first month of the school year, teachers have to engage with students in a way that lets the students get to know who the teacher is and what they stand for. Teachers need to take the time to research their students (look through those cumulative folders) and provide students with information about who they are personally that is both relevant and meaningful. This means sharing photos, family artifacts, likes and dislikes, hobbies, and interest. Students are fascinated with who their teachers are, at least initially.

It is important that you move from stranger to scholar to teacher as quickly as possible. You reveal to your students who you are and what you think of them by:

- How you set up your classroom,
- How you greet and speak about students,
- How you communicate with families and guardians,
- What you bring to share about yourself,
- What images you have on the wall,
- What books you have on the shelves,
- What materials you make available to students,
- What you choose to spend time on and talk about,
- What you read to them, and
- How you play with them.

These elements all help achieve the goal of becoming less of a stranger to a new group of young people with their diverse backgrounds, interests, wonders, and personalities. You must have regular parts of the day when you can just be with the students, engaging with them in the things they like to do. Many teachers call it "choice time."

In the early part of the year, the prosocial community building moments must take priority over the curricular moments in order to build toward a restorative culture in the classroom. As the year progresses and relationships become more established, the community building reduces, though it is always present. Your relationships with your students begin to serve as a lever to keep students engaged through the ebbs and flows of interest in the subject matter content. You are no longer a stranger. You are their teacher.

A PLACE IN THE CLASSROOM

The first day of school can be daunting for a first grader. Sometimes there are tears; sometimes apprehension about who they should be and who they are with. Then, there is the question of community and belonging. Ebony Edwards, a first grade teacher at Mt. Clara Elementary School, meets her students on the schoolyard at 8:25 a.m. on the first day, grinning ear to ear, excited about the possibilities for her young students.

She looks down the line to see one of the most diverse groups of students she has ever met. Black. Brown. Honeysuckle. Light-skinned to a rich blue-black. All these new faces. All these new relationships. All wondering what she will be like. And who is this stranger with whom their parents have left them? They are mapping the image of the Ms. Edwards before them and the potential of who she could be, against their own experiences of "the teacher." Some will have only their parents as a reference, but most will have a string of other adults and teachers with which to compare and build those expectations upon.

She smiles and gestures for them to follow her, reaching out her hand to the student at the head of the line, who takes it with hesitation and allows this stranger, who they are learning to trust, to lead the line up to the classroom.

She smiles and greets other students and families as they move through the hall, giving hugs and accepting hugs all along the way. The line stops at the top of each landing in the stairwell to be sure everyone is with them. Ms. Edwards smiles and says, "good job everyone!," being sure to look at and acknowledge each student; ensuring that her first interactions with them are not telling them what to do, but rather expressions of joy that they are *her* students and she is happy to see them. She starts every day this way, trying to leave no doubt for students that this is exactly where she wants to be and they are who she wants to be with.

At the door of the classroom, Ms. Edwards tells them how she wants them to enter and what she wants them to do. "Go in quietly, hang your things up, and find a place in the classroom to read. You can read by yourself or you can partner with a friend. You may also talk quietly, but have a book to share with each other."

The classroom is organized into several student-centered areas, each for a specific purpose and use for the students. When entering the room there is a sense of warmth. There are three large rugs that create a soft space for the students to sit and spend time. There are many plants placed around the room. The library is organized and filled with books with a wide collection of characters, topics, and themes, fiction and nonfiction. Books are abundant and available for students to peruse at their leisure. Many students quickly find books that suit their interests, and they settle into a place to read. Some students are drawn to each other, while others read by themselves.

This soft landing in the room invites students to enter and engage with tasks and people that they find enjoyable, while exercising their personal agencies. This gives the teacher time to engage with parents and check in individually with students to help them transition from the energy of home to the energy of the classroom space.

After 15–20 minutes, everyone is invited to come to the library for Ms. Edwards to share a story with them. The students come over eagerly, curious as to what she will share. The first book she chooses is a self-published text about her own life and journey to becoming a teacher. In the book, she writes about her family and talks about the schools she attended and the jobs she has had. In his book, she also shares about losing his mother.

One of the students comes up afterward and takes her hand and says, "Ms. Edwards, I am sorry you lost your mother. Are you still sad? My goldfish died last week. I'm still sad about it, but I think we will be ok."

In her book, the teacher shares moments of joy and success, as well as loss and struggle. Her students are incredibly engaged and interested in who Ms. Edwards is outside of the classroom and how she talks about herself and her experiences. They want to know what moves her and what makes her vulnerable. By the end of the first day, Ms. Edwards is less of a stranger than when the day began.

LET'S CIRCLE UP!

After the story, the class moves to their learning circle, which is an area rug big enough for all the students and teacher to sit together, legs crossed, around its edge. Ms. Edwards greets the students with a "good morning, students," to which they respond, "good morning, Ms. Edwards." She starts the circle with a review of the activities for the day, answering any student questions about what is in store for the day. Afterward, she takes out a talking stick to begin a more formal circle to allow students to introduce and share a little bit about themselves.

Establishing daily circles in your elementary school classroom routines are essential to building a climate that supports restorative practices. At the start of each day, it is essential to have a time when you come together, both to get to know each other and to help students anticipate what to expect from the day. Some teachers will even do two a day, one in the morning after students get settled and another right after lunch, which is often the longest period in the day when the students are not with the teacher.

There are seven main types of circles used in most elementary school classrooms, each with a different purpose, level of student engagement, facilitation, and focus.

1. **Check-In/Agenda Review Circle** (Frequency: one to two times a day) In the check-in/agenda review circle, the teacher welcomes the students: "Hello, class. How are you? Today we will be . . . ." There is also a question-and-answer component to allow students to ask any questions they may have about the agenda and what they can expect. This can take anywhere from 5–15 minutes, depending on the length of the question-and-answer, and is often used to build anticipation and remind students of behavior norms and expectations.

2. **Sharing Circle** (Frequency: one to two times a week) There is usually a prompt for students to answer and a talking piece that students hold to symbolize they are the speaker. There is no dialogue. Each student responds to the prompt, and the talking piece is passed from person to person around the circle. Sentence frames are incredibly helpful, especially for English language learner students. Everyone has equal time to speak and share one to two things with the group. Active listening and being a "good audience" are stressed here. Having one's experiences heard and validated, as well as likes and dislikes, are also an important focus.

3. **Risk Taking/Social Sharing Circle** (Frequency: one to two times a week) This structure is similar to the sharing circle, but the questions go deeper and require more vulnerability on the part of the students.

4. **Community Building Circles** (Frequency: one per day in the first few months of school, then two to three times per week for the remainder of the school year) These circles include various group activities and ice breakers specifically designed to build community amongst the students and with the teacher.

5. **Demonstration Circle** (Frequency: one per week) In this circle, an object is shared with the group, and students are encouraged to ask questions, touch, feel, and explore the object. Handling materials/objects and taking care with other people's things are stressed. This is

often done before an activity where students will get to engage with similar objects. However, sometimes this is an activity unto itself.

6. **Processing/Debrief Circle** (Frequency: as often as needed—no more than two times per day) This circle is essential for hearing feedback and responding to a shared event or experience within the class. It is also a space to surface concerns and lingering feelings students may have about an event, activity, or shared experience. Some students will share and some may not. There may be some back and forth, but students are expected to share only about the topic/event/activity that occurred.

7. **Accountability Circle** (Frequency: use sparingly, as it is very time consuming) This is a high-level, high-stakes type of circle where everyone's attention is brought to a few students to help challenge, push, or support those students.

Each type of circle has specific goals and skill sets that it utilizes and nurtures, all with the goal of building community in the classroom. Leading circles on a daily basis serves a dual role of building community and creating a structure for resolving conflict that everyone is familiar with and comfortable in.

Circles are powerful spaces for students when resolving conflicts because, whether they caused the harm or were impacted by it, they will associate circles with joyful moments, a sense of being heard and belonging, and a feeling of empowerment. This will give them an extra support in navigating challenging conversations and confrontations. Team building exercises and classroom experiences that contribute to positive relationships, such as assemblies, field trips, group projects, and singing together, also contribute to building classroom community.

WHEN CONFLICT HAPPENS: THE EMOTION DETECTIVE OR WAS IT AN ACCIDENT?

As conflicts arise in the elementary classroom, the teacher must intervene as soon as he or she becomes aware of it. Immediately, students should begin to engage in the restorative process. This does not mean that everything has to be resolved in that moment, but the process must start and progress to a calm and stable place before students are allowed to engage again or go about their way. There are three important aspects of this part of the restorative process: finding the truth, recognizing the impact, and brainstorming a different outcome and the apology.

How these steps are handled is critical in getting to the restorative outcome you want. When teachers are present to witness the conflict, it is easier to know the facts of what happened, but getting to the motivations and feelings involved requires a more involved conversation with students. That conversation should ask the students to articulate the facts for themselves before looking at who was harmed or impacted. If the teacher is not present for the start of the conflict, then they must find out who was involved and engage each student separately to find out what happened and how they felt at the time, before bringing them together.

In finding the truth of any conflict with elementary students, you have to know not only the facts of what was done but also what happened emotionally for all involved. If the emotional arc does not match the facts of what happened, you know there is more to the story, and you must continue to ask questions of students to help them get to the core of their conflict. "What were you thinking and feeling at the time?" is the essential restorative question at this stage of the process.

It is important during this step that teachers do not project their own emotions onto students or lighten the truth of their students' actions or motivations. It can be tempting to tell young students that it was an accident when something bad happens to them or when someone does something to harm them. However, teachers should only call incidents accidents that are actually accidents and should help students properly name their emotions and feelings.

Elementary students may not have the language to describe their emotions, but their emotions do impact them just as deeply as adults. Children, like adults, sometimes act out of jealousy, greed, or anger. It is important to help them name it and understand it before we take steps to help them take responsibility and move on from the situation. One tool that we use is having an illustrated emotions chart. This is also great for English language learners who may not have the language skills but can point out how they are feeling.

For students to truly be able to take responsibility for their actions, they need to recognize who is impacted by their choices and any harm that came from it. Elementary students are developmentally in a place where they need significantly more guidance in discovering what results come from the choices they make and who is impacted by them.

Depending on the behaviors and resulting harm for older elementary school students, you have to talk about direct and indirect impacts and principal actors and witnesses, and students must be responsible for making it as right as possible with all involved.

There are two primary goals for the restorative process at this level:

1. Making things as right as possible, and
2. Learning from the experience so that the same harm doesn't happen again.

In order for the second goal to be attained, students need to know another way is possible—that different choices could have been made given what happened and the feelings involved.

Brainstorming with the students involved about the different choices and possible outcomes resulting from those choices helps children gain a sense of agency around their own feelings. It gives students the opportunity to imagine a more prosocial way of engaging with each other and gives them something to draw from in future similar situations. This is best reflected upon and shared before an apology is given so that those impacted are reassured of it not happening again and are more likely to accept the apology as sincere.

"ARE YOU OKAY?" GOES A LONG WAY

One day Ms. Edwards came down to the recess yard early to pick up her students, hoping to get them back up to the classroom to allow enough time to complete a writing project they had been working on for two weeks. When she arrived on the yard, she noticed Milton was sitting on the school's "heart bench," a place for children to self-select to take a break if they have a minor injury or just need to catch their breath. He was crying, so Ms. Edwards went over to investigate. As she approached, Milton rushed over. "Ms. Edwards! Ms. Edwards! Henry hit me for no reason, and he won't let me play kickball with them!"

He burst into a round of sobs. Ms. Edwards reminded Milton that while sometimes people may not want to play with him, which is okay, no one has a right to put their hands on another student.

Ms. Edwards immediately called over Henry and asked Milton if anyone else was involved.

"No!" Milton replied.

Henry arrived with the three other boys he had just been playing with. He saw Milton crying, and the teacher could see his mind racing back to earlier in the recess. Quickly, he resigned himself to having to deal with the situation.

"Yes, Ms. Edwards," said Henry.

"What happened between you and Milton? Can you explain why Milton is upset?"

Henry looked from Milton to Ms. Edwards and shrugged his shoulders as if to say, "I don't know," but then he admitted that he excluded Milton from playing kickball.

"And?" the teacher questioned.

"Uh . . . I . . . uh. I hit him?" he explained hesitantly, his voice in the tone of a question.

"Did you?" Ms. Edwards clarified.

"Yes," he admitted, trying to say as little as possible.

By then, Milton had stopped crying to focus with complete attention on his teacher to see how she would handle the incident. Then, Milton blurted out, part accusation, part whine, "he didn't even say sorry," hoping to increase the amount of "trouble" Henry would be in.

Ms. Edwards reminded Milton to be quiet and respect that Henry was talking. This move served the dual purpose of communicating to Milton and Henry that, even with the possibility of being "in trouble," all students involved deserve respect. This space gave Henry permission to be more open about what happened and what his motivations were.

"Henry, please tell me what happened to make you exclude Milton, especially given that our classroom agreements are to be inclusive. On the yard, we share all the equipment," Ms. Edwards reminded her student. By referencing and reinforcing the classroom shared values on the yard, it was a reminder to all students involved and witnessing that the expectation was to live the values that they had all agreed upon.

Henry went on to explain how at an earlier recess Milton had run into him and knocked him down, causing him to scrape his knee. He was quick to add that Milton did not apologize either. Ms. Edwards turned to Milton now to ask, "Is it true?"

"Yes," the child replied with his eyes just holding back the tears. "It was an accident."

"Did you apologize?" the teacher pushed.

"No," Milton explained and immediately apologized to Henry.

"And?" Edwards said to give Milton the opportunity to remember and practice the steps in the apology frame they have been taught.

"Are you ok?" Milton asked Henry.

Henry responded, "yes" with a nod.

Now Ms. Edwards turned her attention back to Henry, not forgetting that he had both caused harm and was harmed, asking him to continue speaking. "So, Henry, tell me more about what happened and how you felt at the time." This line of questioning kept the conversation focused on Milton and his role and responsibility in holding on to his hurt from earlier and escalating things.

Henry quickly recapped his earlier collision with Milton and then moved on to say, "so at this recess, Milton just came over and was trying to play with us, but I didn't want him to so I said no. And he came close like he was going to try to take the ball, so I hit him by accident. It was an accident," he said, partly pleading to convince Ms. Edwards and Milton both.

Milton, feeling like he wanted to be fair, said to Henry, "That's okay."

Henry's response to call it an "accident" signaled to the teacher that Henry had not accepted his responsibility, though he seemed genuinely interested in making Milton feel better. But he also saw apologizing as a ticket out of trouble because he felt that was how they resolved his conflict with Milton.

Ms. Edwards, having practiced this conversation many times in various situations, decided to unpack it further to help Henry and Milton give words to their emotions and to ensure they accepted responsibility for their roles and behavior in the conflict. She listened to the rest of Henry's and Milton's accounts of what happened and helped them make the distinction between choice and accident. They came to understand that Milton's behavior was a response to what had happened earlier and was very intentional, though the outcome was not anticipated.

In the end, Henry was able to articulate that he chose his actions because of how he felt and that he was responsible for that choice. Part of the final discussion was about what else he could have done with his negative emotions other than hitting. However, the real insight for both students was when they traced the path of emotions to their origin. It was Milton's choice that had precipitated all the subsequent harm. Together, Ms. Edwards and her students had concluded that had Milton simply stopped to say "Are you okay?" to Henry when he knocked him down, no further harm would have occurred.

In Ms. Edwards's elementary classroom, she always stresses that a casual apology is dangerous and rarely enough, but a moment of responsibility and compassion to say, "Are you okay? What do you need?," goes a long way to reducing harm and making things as right as possible.

CONFLICT MANAGERS

Eisha is a fifth grader who has been at her elementary school for six years. Her sister went there before her and her younger sister is now in second grade. Everyone, children and adults alike, knows Eisha. She is generally seen as a quiet, studious, and nice girl. Arabic is the language she speaks at home with her family, and English is her third language.

Almost every day, she makes sure to complete her class work early so that she can be excused to walk down to the little hall closet, converted into a micro-office space. There she dons her stop sign red T-shirt uniform emblazoned with the school's mascot (a dragon) drawn large around the front and the words "Conflict Manager" emboldened in big block letters on the back. Eisha pulls the red T-shirt over her head and feels taller. Her back straightens as she is filled with pride by her new role. She grabs her whistle and slips it around her neck. Next, she straps on her blue fanny pack filled with bandages and her clipboard and notepaper.

Today, she will join ten to fifteen other youth spread across the fourth and fifth grades, all of who went through in-depth training to be able to serve in the capacity as a conflict manager.

Conflict managers are deployed during the recess time to provide eye-level, peer-to-peer intervention and leadership around restorative discipline practices for the entire student body. Conflict managers are trained to utilize five restorative questions:

1. What happened?
2. What were you thinking of at the time?
3. What have you thought of since?
4. Who has been affected by what you have done? In what way?
5. What do you think you need to do to make things right?

Conflict managers are also trained in how to recognize and interrupt bullying. The students are shown a video on bullying and are given the space to talk about their own experiences. Students brainstorm and role-play together the signs and precursors of bullying and what to do about them. They also talk about how they understand relationships and some of the tensions that commonly arise amongst students their age or younger.

The school provides a regular space to talk about what they are seeing, and they have an adult coordinator who is able to facilitate these conversations during their lunch or recess time. Teachers support this work by carving out regular time in the afternoon for students to do accelerated work and participate.

The conflict managers model has had a dramatic effect on student behavior, giving students concrete skills they can apply directly to their own relationships, as well as giving them insight into their own behavior in a way that is transformative.

Jasmin was a student who had transferred to Mt. Clara Elementary School in the third grade. She had an extremely negative experience at her last school, and her mother felt like the school had given up on her daughter, whom she admittedly knew could be difficult. She would say, "I know my daughter can be a bit stubborn and hard-headed. She is just sensitive. But under all her attitude, she has a good heart. She's a good girl like her younger sister."

Jasmin had a younger sister who was placed in the first grade at Mt. Clara Elementary. In spite of her mother's care and the efforts of her teacher, Jasmin still had a rough start. Early on, she was drawn into a conflict with one of the more popular groups of girls at the school. She had a hard time finding her place within the preexisting social relationships that students had built since kindergarten. At the urging of her teacher, during a restorative conference with Jasmin and her mother following an incident that involved name-calling and shoving, Jasmin was encouraged to apply to be a conflict manager.

With the help of her teacher, Jasmin applied and was accepted into the conflict managers' program. The program afforded Jasmin the chance to talk about her experiences and get to know other students, while breaking down some of her social isolation. This also allowed her to utilize her experience to help students get to the heart of their feelings and build healthier relationships.

This leadership development model empowers student to take an active role in shaping the climate at their school. Conflict manager programs are an effective model for extending and integrating restorative discipline practices into an elementary school context in a meaningful and sustainable way.

FLEMING LEADERSHIP SCHOOL: BUILDING UPON AGREEMENTS

Ms. Jansen's third grade class of twenty-four students sat quietly in a large circle at the end of the school day. One by one, the eight- and nine-year-olds were sharing about how Reinaldo's behavior had affected them and how he made them feel. Reinaldo was energetic and uninhibited, characteristics that were often frustrating and challenging for both his teachers and his peers. "When you're on his good side, he can be nice but you do not want to be on his bad side," explains another student in Ms. Jansen's class.

Reinaldo has spent a good part of recess and lunchtime tormenting his peers by slapping them and calling them names. When he hit a girl in his class for no apparent reason, Ms. Jansen decided it was time for a peacemaking circle.

The peacemaking circle is the basic element of the restorative justice program at Fleming Leadership School, a bilingual kindergarten through eighth grade public school in East Oakland. Fleming Leadership School is one of several elementary schools in Oakland dedicated to building, through restorative processes, the socio-emotional skills students needed to navigate conflict and deal with challenging situations.

The school's vision includes the idea that it "will be a place where students can exercise their curiosity, their voice, make meaningful choices and challenge themselves and each other academically and where students develop their sense of responsibility to transform our school, community and world." Additionally, they have developed the following agreements to help guide the interactions of both students and staff:

- We are kind and create safe spaces.
- We teach and learn.

• We take responsibility for ourselves and our community.

After receiving multiple "avisos" for his behavior, Reinaldo was asked to reflect on his behavior and write about it in preparation for the peacemaking circle. For the last hour of the school day, Ms. Jansen's class was transformed into a large circle with all twenty-four students sitting in their tiny chairs facing each other around the room.

The process begins with the facilitator asking four basic questions: What happened? Which agreement was not followed? Who got hurt? and How do we fix the situation? The circle goes in rounds, and each student gets a chance to offer her or his input in response to the questions.

In the peacemaking circle with Reinaldo, he got to hear from almost all of his classmates. Several spoke about being bullied by him and how it made them sad, frustrated, scared, or angry. One girl explained, "Reinaldo kept cutting in front of me, and we have a line order. I asked him to get back in his spot, and he just punched me. Reinaldo, can you please not do that next time. I really didn't like it, and it didn't feel good."

But the power of the circle is not only connected to hearing from those who were harmed. Other students, those who were not slapped or called names by Reinaldo, spoke up about how they felt bad that someone was being mean to their friends or how they got angry at him because he was not being kind. A few important voices also shared how Reinaldo was always nice to them, but how they wished he treated everyone that same way.

After all the other students who wanted to share had spoken, Reinaldo read the reflection he had written and apologized to the whole class. He did not know exactly why he was being so mean to his classmates, but he knew it was not okay and he promised to stop hitting others and calling them names.

STARTING YOUNG AND BUILDING UP

Fleming Leadership School is an elementary school and a middle school, so they have a lot of time to develop the skills and acquire the language necessary to operationalize the restorative process with students. In kindergarten through second grade, the process usually involves only the students directly involved in an incident and is heavily facilitated by the teacher. The focus is on fairness, and the restorative process is still grounded in the three agreements named above, but the attention is almost always given to the first agreement—we are kind and create safe spaces.

At ages five, six, and seven, children really care about what happened *right now*. Often, by the time the restorative process has come to a close, their attention has moved on to something else, and the most serious issue is that they are still being asked to focus on the conversation.

But the school believes the process is still important, even essential because it helps their youngest students practice using the language connected to their agreements. Words such "community" and "responsibility" become more concrete when children talk about them in real and immediate circumstances. And, perhaps most importantly, engaging in the restorative process establishes the expectation that when they have been harmed, have caused harm, or been involved in a situation in which a friend or classmate was harmed, they have some responsibility in making the situation better. An adult does not simply take care of the situation and make it go away.

Starting in third grade at Fleming Leadership School, the students get involved in different ways and begin to take more leadership in the restorative process. This is the age when they start utilizing peacemaking circles, which include other community members beyond those directly involved in an incident. Another critical new step during this phase is that the process begins to ask "who else was involved with and impacted by the situation?"

The conversations and connections to the school's agreements become more sophisticated as students are able to take on more cognitively and emotionally complex ideas and reflections. When asked about the peacemaking circle for Reinaldo in Ms. Jansen's class, one third grader asserted, "we run it by ourselves." That same student was able to articulate how it was important that Reinaldo hear from all the different students in his class, not just the ones he had hit or yelled at.

In middle school, students take on even greater ownership of the restorative process. By then it has become normalized and the expectation has been established that if a student harms another or violates one of the agreements, she or he will be held accountable by others. Ms. Ramirez, the assistant principal at Fleming Leadership School, laughs as she explains how enthusiastic many of her sixth through eighth graders are about their sense of justice. "By the time they come to me they have already gone through the reflective process," she says.

In many cases, the adults serve only as a position of authority with whom the students check in about the restorative process they have undergone independently. This is the true indicator of the success of the restorative model at Fleming Leadership School; it has become an integral part of the culture for both students and teachers. It is not something that takes place outside of the classroom or beyond the playground, in a closed room controlled by a teacher or administrator. Rather, restorative justice is a guide, a tool, and a philosophy for how they treat one another, take responsibility, and build community together.

Chapter Eight

Struggles and Opportunities

Overcoming the Challenges of Implementing a Restorative Model

Authored by Renjitham Alfred and Rekia Jibrin

Gina's eighth grade U.S. history students were expressing hurt and anger about needing to learn about slavery in their classroom. Gina, who was a white teacher, exacerbated these feelings. Gina was actively engaged in practicing restorative justice with her colleagues and taught the restorative justice elective for another group of students. She was open, willing, and actively respectful of the students' perspectives on issues. So when they requested a dialogue, she participated in a restorative circle with them to discuss the issue they had with the class content on slavery. Gina expresses her experience with the restorative justice circle in the text box below.

One of the most meaningful circles I have ever experienced occurred when the restorative justice coordinator approached me to participate in a circle with two of my eighth grade U.S. history students. The students asked the RJ coordinator to hold a circle about my teaching about slavery in the classroom. The students had told the RJ coordinator that they didn't want to hear about American slavery, and that it was especially difficult to be taught by me, a Caucasian.

In the circle, the students expressed how difficult and hurtful it had been for them to be in class for the last couple of days, hearing about slavery in the United States. I empathized with their pain and was open to hearing more from them about how they felt. After they expressed their feelings, I apologized and told them how terrible I felt. I was moved to tears and told them how much I didn't like teaching these lessons and that it was also very painful for me. I explained that I had struggled with how to teach the material and that hurting them was the last thing that I had wanted to do.

The circle then decided that each class would pick examples of enslavement in different parts of the world to study instead of looking specifically at American slavery. After looking at examples from other parts of the world, I moved the class to researching American abolitionists. This has been my practice in teaching this unit ever since. The circle allowed my students and me to speak openly about slavery and to come up with a way of teaching the material that was sensitive, respectful, and broad in its coverage and meaning.

The story above was sent via e-mail from Gina King, then in her second year in the classroom. Her experiences illuminate important components necessary for the implementation of restorative justice in schools by school staff. The circle Gina describes took place a year after her school began to implement restorative justice. Gina was already training and working with other school staff who were practicing restorative justice with each other, reflecting that restorative justice practices start with a healthy adult community. Building off the work of relationship development with the adults in her school, Gina was then able to model the values of adult relationships to her students' unmet needs in the classroom. Her school had a restorative justice coordinator to work with her and her students, and space outside Gina's classroom, but still in the school, was provided.

Gina focused on how the U.S. history curriculum affected a class. Through a restorative process, she had the opportunity to further connect with her students and understand that her students were uncomfortable with the curriculum. They knew Gina was using restorative practices, and they knew she would be open to having a conversation about it. Consequently, Gina's students initiated a restorative dialogue and provided an important historical and emotional context to Gina, which impacted the way she changed her teaching methodology to better meet the needs of her students.

THE CONTEXT

For school staff (including administrators) to think about implementing restorative justice practices in schools, *context* should matter. Culture change in schools cannot be operationalized without the commitment, movement, and consistent continuum of practices led by people (Morrison and Thorsborne 2005). Scholars seeking solutions to school discipline and violence conceptualize discipline and violence using criminalizing or even medicalizing approaches (Edelman 2007; Prothrow-Stith and Spivak 2004; Fagan 2002; Feld 1998).

As is the American social ethic of seeing problems as primarily individual problems, these scholars place the burden of change solely on individuals, such as students, teachers, administrators, or community members. When implementing restorative justice in schools, every person has a part to actively engage, as do their contexts. This chapter invites us to imagine and grapple with the complexities of how to think through implementing restorative justice in schools, based on school and community needs, as well as the needs of the people who work in schools in partnership with communities.

Much of the literature of restorative justice encourages us to think beyond zero tolerance. Data acquired regarding the use of zero tolerance policies show that these policies have harmed schools and made them more unsafe rather than safer, as they were created in the first place (Skiba and Knesting 2002). It describes the need for restorative justice in schools as a solution to punishment that is meted out disproportionately in frequency and severity to students of color and to reduce incidences of bullying (Payne and Welch 2013; Morrison 2007).

Other scholars rightly draw attention to compounding institutional policies that contribute to the school-to-prison pipeline and "the racial discipline gap," which looks at the racialized students' repeated suspension and expulsion creating a higher likelihood of them dropping out of school and into the justice system (Wadhwa 2016; Gregory, Skiba, and Noguera 2010). Besides clear separation practices, such as suspensions and expulsions, the not accounted for practice of sending students out, with or without a written referral, and placing them in in-school suspension rooms denies youth the education they rightly deserve and impairs their academic acquisition and progress.

Restorative justice scholars task us with recognizing that school staff are not working with products but human beings and thus recommend a humanizing approach to culture change and student behaviors in schools, with particular attention to race, mass incarceration, school culture, and student alienation (Wadhwa 2016; Morrison 2007; Hopkins 2003). However, to expect *only* individual educators to disrupt this pipeline and prevent racial achievement gaps stands in tension to the overarching identification that *institutional* policies, practices, and neglect ultimately shape both school staffs' and students' actions every day. It is from this point of view that this chapter emphasizes the importance of *context* when school staff makes considerations about implementing restorative justice in schools.

The authors of this chapter are scholar practitioners who have implemented and evaluated restorative justice practices in schools, respectively. Renjitham Alfred's practice of conceptualizing, training educators, and implementing restorative practices throughout the city of Oakland and the surrounding

Bay Area school districts informs much of the grounding of this chapter, while Rekia Jibrin draws on her involvement in qualitative evaluation of restorative justice within the high school context in Oakland, California.

Why does *context* matter? School staff working in low-income, resource-poor schools must understand the challenges that can arise while working within a context of poverty and systematic economic deprivation, personal, familial, and neighborhood trauma, underfunded and understaffed schools, over-policed communities, and an ambivalent, if not an overt lack of, administrative district support. Some teachers teach in a restorative way, and for others, Band-Aids© become the go-to response, while a pervasive societal culture of shaming and blaming school staff breeds toxicity in schools.

Teachers need support in schools—on a professional and institutional level—to work with families, to work with students, and to work with each other. Work environment challenges can and should never be divorced from the broader institutional context in which teachers are fighting to keep schools open, to keep their jobs, for smaller classrooms, and for better pay that reflects a valuing of their role in school communities. Furthermore, within the broader societal context, parents are not valued for raising the next generation of workers and citizens and are having to fight for recognition and to be valued for their contribution to society. They also need economic and other social support.

Mass incarceration and the evisceration of social provision in poor communities have taken a serious toll on work opportunities, housing availability and stability, and the constant surveillance of poor peoples' everyday lives (Rios 2011; Alexander 2010; Gilmore 2007; Harvey 2005). Schools themselves are operating under the assault of corporate power that threatens the very existence of public schools themselves, the strength of teachers' unions, racial progress, and our very notion of democracy (Watkins 2012).

It is within this context that children are going to school—a context that blindly accepts color-blind, meritocratic notions of social mobility in a world where class and race do matter because, in fact, very few opportunities exist for the poorest children who need our most focused attention (Watkins 1994). We frame the implementation of restorative justice within this context because we believe it enables educators (and policy makers) to get real about both the challenges and possibilities for transformative social change that our children deserve.

The possibilities of successfully teaching children, especially those who have experienced the marginalization of schooling over time, hinge on the backbone of restorative justice—a model within which proactive, preventative, and consistent relationships are necessary. As explored in chapter 4, restorative justice institutionalizes relationship-building practices in schools and offers a toolbox for staff who wish to build and connect with students. These relationships have profound implications for students' desire to learn and believe in themselves, and for parents' involvement in their children's school experience. Value must be placed by school staff on building upon this involvement in productive and family-centered ways.

Moreover, teachers who successfully implement restorative practices in classrooms believe that they must form more real connections to their colleagues and students that increase the likelihood of students' classroom participation and the importance generated from their perception that their teachers' value them. As parents and students feel seen, teachers themselves who receive relevant teacher training around restorative justice, which acknowledges and values their backgrounds, skills, and insights and nurtures their professional development, also are seen.

Furthermore, teachers who employ and are involved in restorative practices begin themselves to think beyond the punitive paradigm; they begin to envision alternatives to punishment and legal approaches, as well as to rely less on school security, thereby reinvesting forms of teacher sovereignty in classrooms that historically preceded the introduction of school security (Devine 1996).

Relationship building and school culture change take time and concrete support. Much of our practice and research with educators demonstrates that the relationships that school staff themselves build amongst and between each other mirrors possibilities for successful relationship building with their students. Students watch everything, and educators know that students watch how educators interact with each other. When administrators support their teachers, and receive support themselves, strong, positive, and healthy relationships are built on a foundation that recognizes class, gender, and racial difference.

All too often, new teachers experience the intense shock of the realities of poverty, violence, and trauma in struggling communities of color; this shock stems from the fact that so many new teachers do not come from the communities where they work. Restorative justice practices enable teachers to build with one another, to confront and understand questions of power, race, gendered difference, as well as histories of oppression and political struggles in communities that now experience dire forms of social suffocation.

Frequently, because of funding stipulations or even funding availability, the implementation of restorative justice is rapidly sped up with unrealistic expectations of change placed on teachers and students. The realistic implementation of restorative justice fundamentally calls for a prioritizing of the realities of school needs with real expectations for change. How this happens requires a noncompromising stance from grassroots efforts to mobilize political change at city, state, and federal level, as well as at the foundational level, where a systems-based approach to school transformation takes precedence over an outcomes-based approach defined by funders (INCITE 2007).

Additionally, restorative justice structures must be implemented consistently over time. In the context of the rapid reform culture of public education and the reality of frequent teacher and administrator turnover, lack of consistency is one of the most common factors contributing to unsuccessful restorative justice attempts in schools. Even at some of the schools written about in previous chapters, the departure of a few key staff members who held much of the responsibility for restorative justice structures led to the breakdown of schoolwide systems or the loss of specific elements of the restorative justice model.

Trusting the process of implementing restorative justice rests on real expectations set by school staff, teachers, students, and parents in an organic process of envisioning how they wish to utilize restorative practices to best serve school needs. This organic process is contingent upon an alignment of financial and political support by school and district leadership. All too often, mandates for the implementation of restorative justice are set by school district or administrative staff who spend little to no time in classrooms, with students, or with community members. While the rhetoric for restorative justice exists, so, too, does the rhetoric for criminalizing discipline.

This contradiction of institutional practice requires urgent attention. Parent, student, and school-community trust cannot be built when school districts, who say they are for restorative justice, overfund school police units and authorize in-school criminal detainment, arrest, and student questioning in the absence of their parents' presence (Black Organizing Project, Public Counsel, and ACLU 2013). In work conversations with students, school staff, teachers, and parents, the normalization of disrespect and violence has been seen not solely as student behavioral issues learned at home or on the street, but identified and rooted in cultures of disrespect employed by school districts, the police, the court system, and even social services agencies *toward* poor people and their communities (Rios 2011).

School staff know that to place solutions to violence and poverty solely on the shoulders of schools is at best unfair and at worst an eschewing of the responsibility of democratically elected officials who sustain forms of community abandonment through punitive economic and social policies (Gilmore 2008). Even so, schools mirror the societies in which we live, and issues of racism, oppression, and exclusion structure student and teacher experiences in schools. Inexperienced teachers who need and deserve support typically staff poor schools. These teachers, who are all too often racially or economically alienated from their students, are barely prepared for the challenges of the classroom much less mistrust they may or may not encounter from community members in the schools where they teach. As such, the need for a class and a race informed paradigm of restorative justice is critical.

Beyond framing restorative justice as a solution to disproportionate racial discipline, grounding restorative justice as a community-informed approach within schools matters. School staff, especially school security officers, who typically come from the same communities as students and see their duty as keeping schools safe, may perceive restorative justice as an inferior or culturally disconnected form of discipline. For them (and many teachers), the easiest way to discipline a student is to remove them from the school. When no alternatives are presented, many parents also default to hold this view.

The perception of restorative justice as "soft discipline" raises important racial and class differences around child-rearing, around consequences for school misbehavior, and about parents' and school staff's perceptions of how "in control" administrators are in creating safe schools. Furthermore, when restorative justice is introduced only as an alternative to discipline, as a way to reduce suspensions, it paves the way for school staff disillusionment when there is no rapid change in student behavior.

The issue of setting clear, firm consequences for harmful behavior invariably structures the way school communities believe they should hold students accountable. The confrontation of outsider-insider philosophies of justice and discipline are critical racial, class-based, and cultural issues that must be addressed in implementing restorative justice. The danger of bringing in a philosophy and practice that disregards the ways communities handle conflict is quite dire (Barganier and Jibrin 2016).

Mistrust of the restorative process can result in silencing dissent from community voices that challenge the process, and this requires skilled negotiations between community-based workers and school members who can both incorporate community values within the restorative justice practice and aligning those values to school ones. The seeming abstractness of this process still relies on the concrete belief that implementing restorative justice from a grounded racial justice paradigm offers commonsense alternatives to an overreliance on forms of legal processes that alienate communities and tear apart relationships rather than providing adequate resources, support, and instruction needed.

If restorative justice is perceived as "soft" in its implementation and the training of its implementation, then the fidelity to the practice that demands true accountability is missing. Some school staff, parents, and students perceive restorative justice processes as much more tedious and emotionally involved than typical discipline. In American culture, individual stoicism is typically seen as the norm, while emotionality is seen as weakness.

Restorative justice processes go against our societal norms. Doing this *is* a change in how we relate to each other because it goes precisely counter to alienating ethics of individualism, competition, and consumption instilled by an American meritocratic mentality that erases embedded practices of racism, classism, and patriarchy within institutional structures that perpetuate a racial caste system (Alexander 2010). Restorative justice practices redeem dignity and humanity in relationships, typically degraded by separation and exclusion in schools. Teachers come to this profession wanting to reach across this divide and have every child succeed. Teachers typically come into teaching because they love children or the content of what they teach. But they don't have the energy to think about what it means to be interconnected. They are always thinking about their production as workers based on standards and can barely think about context. How do we introduce them to context and give them the support they need?

MAKING RESTORATIVE JUSTICE PRACTICES A POSSIBILITY IN THE CLASSROOM

When school staff is expected to adopt restorative justice practices, they may feel stressed out and at a loss. These practices begin with adults because it is the adults who hold the schools' cultures. Practicing restorative justice allows adults the space to learn and grow as well. There is a concern about the well-being of our teachers who are overburdened, stressed out, and exhausted; teachers who need to be acknowledged for their capacities and their blind spots. They need experiential training to challenge them on their perspectives and world views that may counter those of the students they teach. Coming to a decision-making consensus around what values there are and the ways these values play out in a school community continues a deepening of relationships. Restorative justice practices start with a healthy adult community.

The ways they practice these relationships amongst themselves as adults allows them to form these relationships with students, modeling these relationships on values of openness, patience, and curiosity, rather than judgment, and to question the inappropriate behavior of children as related to unmet needs (Kidde and Alfred 2011). As one teacher aptly put it:

I think, perhaps, a lot of discipline problems would disappear if—I think kids need to feel like we as a society value them. And that the school, society, that we're investing in them, and we care, and we want to make their high school as good of an experience as it is for more affluent kids. It's very important to respect the kids as human beings, and for them to know that you respect them. And the way to do that is through caring . . . you have to. . . . It's subtle . . . they have to believe that you care about them.

When there are structured opportunities for teachers to build relationships with each other, the relationships that get built make it safer for them to look at conflicts with each other and the unmet needs that produce the conflict. Teachers have to know what is expected of them around the practice of implementing restorative justice rather than being forced under unclear mandates from top-level bureaucracy that places the burden of addressing disparities and disproportionate suspension on teachers.

For teachers to be able to adopt and implement restorative justice requires systems that take into account the *time* and *skills* needed for the facilitation of these processes. Time may involve the negotiation of reducing instructional minutes or repurposing class periods, such as advisory periods, while skills involve content-related areas and experiential training before actual implementation occurs in classrooms (Hopkins 2003). Teachers can lead community building in classrooms, but when there is a conflict where a dedication of more time is needed outside the classroom, the resource of additional space is needed. Other *resources* could include a restorative justice coordinator who can actually facilitate the process, a restorative justice coach who can provide continual learning support and troubleshoot challenges of classroom implementation, and a dedicated space outside of the classroom in their school building for restorative justice practices to take place.

If teachers, students, parents, and school communities understand that restorative justice is built on complex interconnections between peoples' histories, cosmologies, and school experiences, this allows for a more contextual and supportive approach to school transformation.

Chapter Nine

Adult Restorative Circles and Adult Reflection

Teachers Building a Foundation of Community

In their excellent book *Leadership on the Line*, Heifetz and Linsky (2002) assert the primacy of professional relationships, "The nature and quality of the connection human beings have with each other is more important than almost any other factor in determining results" (75). This is as true of the functioning of schools as it is of any other business, organization, or institution. However, schools and teachers, especially those serving poor and marginalized communities in this country, face the dilemma of always having more work to do than they have time and resources to accomplish these tasks.

Teachers are notoriously overworked and underpaid. Schools are notoriously overburdened with fixing the ills of a broader society. So it is no surprise that amidst the wave of priorities—improving test scores, backward mapping the next unit, family conferences, schoolwide literacy initiatives, planning field trips, aligning learning targets to the Common Core, and grading essays—few schools build in the time to tend to adult relationships as part of their routine professional development plan.

Nonetheless, if we believe Heifetz and Linsky, and staff lunchrooms and copy machine conversations across the country provide evidence to do so, schools must find ways to nurture a sense of respect and community among staff members if they are going to generate high levels of academic success for all students. Adult restorative circles and adult reflection are two tested structures that provide the opportunity for adults to do the work and relationship building that they ask their students to do on a continual basis—work necessary for a highly functional school and, in turn, highly successful students. The trials, tribulations, discoveries, and unfinished progress of three schools in Oakland will help bring to light the importance of committing to relationship development among staff.

ADULT REFLECTION

In the same way building relationships and seeking to understand where students are coming from are preventative justice measures intended to address problems with student discipline before they arise, adult reflection is a preventative structure for avoiding negative or destructive staff culture.

Rise Up High School is a small school with an aspirational vision of what it means to educate young people in East Oakland's Fruitvale district. The staff consists of passionate, dedicated educators who are profoundly committed to social justice and ensuring the success of their young people. They work hard, care deeply, and hold a sincere sense of responsibility for their school and their community. These are all characteristics that any school leader would look for in her staff. However, they are also the makings of challenging adult dynamics, a reality that, despite the positive intentions of the adults in the building, has at times contaminated the fabric of Rise Up High School, impacting the energy in the building and, ultimately, the experience of the students.

Mark is one of the most well-liked teachers in the school. His stance is urgent and demanding and his classroom is high-energy, relevant, and engaging. On any given day you can enter his classroom and observe his students analyzing Kendrick Lamar lyrics, identifying counternarratives about their communities, or discussing the qualities of effective leadership. He is a pillar of the school community and has worked hard to build this foundation. He loves Rise Up High School. But this love is at times expressed in ways that are damaging or disparaging to other adults in the school community, those who Mark does not believe are working hard enough or acting in alignment with his vision.

Josefina is the epitome of a warm demander in the classroom. Students step up to the level of rigor and expectation in her class because she demands it in a way that communicates how intensely she cares for them and their success. Having grown up in Oakland herself, she understands in a way that most teachers do not the struggles and barriers facing Rise Up students every day, which is why she chooses year after year to return to teach at the school, despite being frustrated by the ways she sees the school failing to fully serve its students. Like Mark, she loves Rise Up High School. But she is also exhausted by giving all of herself and not experiencing the improvements she hopes for.

Lorena has been teaching longer than almost anyone else on staff. Her passion for teaching literature is equaled only by her care for her students. In many ways, she is the embodiment of the school's mission of growing skilled, knowledgeable, critically conscious, and reflective leaders. Although she grew up and first taught in Los Angeles, Oakland is her chosen home and the community to which she feels a powerful sense of commitment. And like Mark and Josefina, Lorena's dedication to her school and students is accompanied by high expectations of everyone around her, expectations that can leave little room for fellow staff members to hold different views or make mistakes.

Rise Up, like all schools, is a living organism in a perpetual process of change and transition. Although the mission is well-established and there are firm structures and systems in place that guide how the school operates, including an agreed upon set of core values, every adult in the building brings with her or him a set of beliefs, ideals, skills, and experiences that influences her or his conception of the most effective way to reach this mission. The seriousness that Mark, Josefina, and Lorena bring to their work, an urgency shared by many of the teachers at Rise Up High School, and at schools throughout the country, is a powerful asset. However, it can also be the source of intense conflict.

If you have been around teachers with such a sense of urgency, you know that conversations as basic as a school's hat policy or whether or not to allow food in the classroom can get heated and that solutions are not easily found. It follows that major issues, such as a school's grading expectations or the focus of professional development, can be completely overwhelming to the degree that if staff members are not able to understand each other and communicate in a productive and respectful way, the school can be torn apart.

One structure that several schools around the Bay Area, including Rise Up High School, have used to address adult conflict, both before and after it occurs, is adult reflection. Adult reflection is a specific and highly organized model for facilitated whole-staff professional development, focused on adult relationships and developed by two non-profit organizations, On the Move and Alternatives in Action. According to the "Adult Reflection Elements" guide (2004) developed by these two organizations:

> Adult Reflection is a practice designed to produce individual and system-wide change in organizations. Its purpose is to create a space where staff members learn to support and challenge each other in their professional and personal development. Ultimately, that support spreads throughout the day-to-day work, establishing a culture of learning and human development. Consequently, AR is intended for organizations striving to become, or remain, "learning organizations." We define a learning organization as a group of individuals working toward a common set of goals and committed to the following values:

- Cultivating curiosity and the capacity to question assumptions
- Being creative and adaptive
- Working as a team in which all members teach and learn from one another, regardless of position, rank, amount of experience, or type of credentials
- Nurturing and sustaining a sense of emotional safety and support
- Encouraging risk-taking as part of everyone's daily work
- Seeking out and addressing tensions and contradictions within the organization
- Acting from an awareness that the personal and the professional are inextricably intertwined
- Building and fostering meaningful relationships with each other
- Investing time and focused attention on each other's professional and personal growth

At Rise Up High School, adult reflection was introduced as a structure in the middle of the year in response to a growing discontent on the part of teachers, which was leading to a damaging divide between teachers and the administration. Distrust was high: some staff members were questioning the intentions and abilities of others, and resentment was developing. It had arrived at the point where some teachers were questioning whether or not they would return the following year because they did not have confidence that Rise Up was moving in the right direction. To accentuate the strain on the community, few of these critical conversations were happening out in the open and with the people who were most impacted by the disapproval. In a school that does not even have a staffroom, the staffroom conversation was fervent.

The adult reflection process at Rise Up began with the Leaders' Circle, a small group of teachers and staff who held various positions of leadership at the school. When the structure was proposed, most members of the Leaders' Circle welcomed it as a necessary step to address the various adult conflicts. "What took us so long to get here?" was a response that exemplifies the feelings of a majority of the participants. There were a few teachers who pushed back because they did not trust that adult reflection would change anything, but they agreed to engage the process because "something needed to change."

Below is a brief overview of the adult reflection process from the On the Move "Adult Reflection Elements" guide (2004):

> Most Adult Reflection groups meet twice a month for a consistent amount of time—generally 90 or 120 minutes. Groups are expected to be punctual— beginning and ending very promptly on time. This expectation is initially set by the Facilitator, but very quickly becomes a group norm. Groups range in size from 6 to 15 members, with an ideal size of about 9 people. Before the meeting time, the Facilitator arranges the chairs in a circle with no table in between. At the starting time, everyone is invited to "check-in." While check-

ins do not proceed in any prescribed order (people moving clockwise around the circle), underlying structures are in place.

Once the check-ins are complete the AR session moves into an "open space," a combination of silence and dialogue in which the actual Reflection takes place. The group may be silent and wait for someone to offer something to explore or the Facilitator may offer a theme or question to begin the dialogue. As we will discuss in the next section, there are important reasons for the Facilitator to consider holding back their initiating comments and allow the group to find its own way. After some moments, dialogue ensues. Every participant checks in, people agree not to respond immediately to other's check-ins, and the Facilitator generally checks-in last.

As each reflector adds his or her voice to the room, questions and themes surface that can become grist for the mill in Reflection. Sometimes a theme arises that is compelling to the group as a whole. Often, time ends up focused on the personal circumstances of one individual at a time. A person is confused about something. They are frustrated, hurt, experiencing change or have perceptions or assumptions they are wrestling with. When the Facilitator raises questions from a place of "authentic curiosity," then they help the reflectors sift through the murkiness or bring forward contradictory sentiments.

The Facilitator keeps an eye on time to ensure that reflectors are not too deep into a subject or issue at the end of the session. This may mean moving the group away from a "hot" discourse as time is ending or choosing not to ask a question that may lead to a longer discourse when only fifteen minutes remain. The Facilitator then moves the group to end, with some time (anywhere from 5 to 10 minutes) set aside for the ritual of acknowledgments.

To close Reflection, the group moves into "acknowledgments." Anyone who wishes is invited to acknowledge behaviors and insights about others in the group. Acknowledgments remind everyone of the intention to create a culture of generosity and appreciation. These offerings most often refer to circumstances that took place within the Reflection section, though they may refer to events in the work environment outside Reflection. (4–6) (See textbox 9.1 for a list of the basic elements of adult reflection.)

Basic Elements of an Adult Reflection Session

Every time a group meets for reflection, the circumstances that play out are unique, as are the specific skills and actions required by the facilitator. Despite the dynamism of each session, there are commonalities that exist in nearly every meeting. Listed below is an overview of some of the most prominent elements of adult reflection.

Authentic Curiosity: The facilitator and the group members ask questions from a place of authentic curiosity, meaning that the asker truly doesn't know the answer to the question posed. Authentically curious questions serve the individual being spoken to and deepen the group's process. Authentic curiosity stands apart from leading questions, in which the asker is actually trying to suggest an answer by asking a question. Questions that come from a place of authentic curiosity do not imply or contain criticism or judgment. Open-ended questions like "how is that working for you?" can lead to places that neither the asker nor the responder could predict.

Facilitator: The facilitator of adult reflection (AR) is often referred to as the "Provocatator." Unlike facilitators in other types of meetings, the AR facilitator does not attempt to make the process smooth or easy, to ease tension, to reduce discomfort, or to ensure equal amounts of participation by all present. The facilitator seeks to name what is in the room and delve more deeply into it. This requires a willingness on the facilitator's part to lead the group into emotionally charged, tense, or uncertain territory.

Agreements: While AR groups do not follow a set of rules, agreements are key to the reflection's success over time. Some of these agreements are required—the facilitator will not start an AR group unless potential participants agree to meet on a regular basis, to sit together, and to arrive and conclude on time. Group members are likely to come to other agreements—cell phones will be turned off; people should allow a couple seconds of quiet before following up another person's comments; try to use the restroom before a session begins. Ultimately, each group comes to a consensus as opposed to being imposed by the facilitator or an administrator.

Confidentiality: Among the agreements expected of all participants is confidentiality. In the simplest terms, what is said in the room stays between those in the room. Conversations will undoubtedly take place after each AR session. However, all participants must commit not to share any information disclosed by individuals with people who are not group members.

Check-in: At the beginning of an AR session, participants bring their voices into the room by describing what they are experiencing in the immediate moment. Since checking-in differs from catching-up, each person's check-in is meant ideally to speak to the present moment. They may reflect back on preceding days or hours, but ultimately check-in is not about bringing members up to speed on recent life events. Any history provided is only to shed light on where a member is right now. Each group member checks in based on what is compelling to him or her. Some may simply say, "I'm here," while others may have stories to tell. While there is no "rule" about the length of a check-in, each reflector is encouraged to be as brief as possible. At the same time, they are also encouraged to invest as much time as necessary to be able to say, "I'm here."

Open Space: "Space" is a useful, yet limited metaphor for the work of reflection. The space that the facilitator holds "open" in the sense that there is no particular direction for the reflection participants to go, no specific topics required for them to address. This is the reflection component of adult reflection, during which any participant may voice a concern, raise questions, or personal issues for other participants to delve into. Open space takes place immediately after the check-in and precedes acknowledgments.

Listening: The facilitator models a listening practice. Hopefully, over time each member of the group begins to pay more attention to what is said by others. Listening is not limited to the explicit stories being told, but also includes paying attention to body language, facial expressions, silence, and use of language.

Language: Observing and reflecting back to the speaker and their use of language is a key facet of the AR facilitator's role (a whole section is devoted to this topic). When they speak, reflectors express a wide range of self-perceptions, metaphors, assumptions, repeated words, and contradictions. Each of these occurrences serves as a window into the deeper workings of the individual speaking.

Energy: Though at times more subtle than the use of language, the facilitator pays close attention to the "energy" in the room. Energy may seem like a nebulous notion, but in fact, it has a very concrete quality to it. The energy in any given moment may be generated by the person speaking, though often more important energy is demonstrated by what goes unsaid. Each participant's body language, silence, facial expressions, squirming, and the tenor of their language all point to underlying energy. The group as a whole tends to hold a common energy—the group may at times be flat, frenetic, intense, silly, excited, focused, distracted, bored, annoyed, or restrained. Generally, there is some quality of tension to the group.

Figure and Ground: This concept drawn from Gestalt therapy helps describe the multilayered dynamics of human interaction. The "ground" is made up of elements in a situation that we are aware of (perhaps peripherally) but are not explicitly paying attention to. For instance, an AR facilitator may be aware of a reflector tapping her foot, but unless the facilitator or another reflector calls attention to the foot tapping, it will not become fodder for discussion. If the facilitator does decide to ask that person, "Why are you tapping your foot?" then the foot tapping becomes figural—meaning that the group is now focused in on the act. In adult reflection, as we sit together, what we call attention to is "figural"—or whatever is coming out of the "ground" at any particular moment. What's figural to one person may not be to another. The question as the facilitator is—what figures do we bring attention to and why? This is the constant choice implicit in adult reflection. What is important isn't which path the facilitator chooses (whether or not to ask about the foot tapping) but that the group stay present and honest to what is figural at the moment.

Tension: Tension in our society is generally viewed as something best avoided or relieved. While tension may not be comfortable, it is a vital component of AR. Tension occurs when there is conflict, or dissonance, within ourselves or between two or more people. Effective action is almost always rooted in creative tension. When the basic agreements of AR are followed, tension inevitably arises within the group. When tension is absent, the facilitator will listen to language, read the energy, and notice the tension that is being withheld.

Hotseat: Often the group focuses on one member of the group for an extended time. For this member, the experience is identified as "sitting on the hotseat." When a person is on the hotseat, he or she is treated with great respect and support. The story or issue that they are presenting is explored through purposeful questioning. Group members may make simple observations of what they are hearing or provide other feedback that helps bring clarity or insight. Within a single AR session, it is not uncommon for only one person to find himself or herself on the hotseat. In other reflection, two or more people may be the focal points over the course of the reflection.

Acknowledgments: For the final five to ten minutes of each session, group members are invited to acknowledge one another. No one is required to offer acknowledgments. Common acknowledgments include recognition for people who were on the hotseat, people who discovered or shared something new about themselves, people who offered support for someone in the group, or someone that is providing leadership. Acknowledgments, at times, are also offered for events that took place out of reflection or in rare occurrences for people not participating in reflection.

© Alternatives In Action, Edd Conboy & On The Move, 2004

"IT'S JUST WHAT WE DO"

United for Change Charter School is a ninth through twelfth grade school in the East Bay where adult reflection has been a foundational practice for several years. Every month, the entire staff engages in the two- to three-hour process with the purpose of "using direct and honest communication among all staff members to create the conditions for a highly functional staff that models the behavior we want to see in our students," according to Leo, one former teacher leader and principal at United for Change. Katie, another teacher, added, "AR is a container for people to have the space to reflect on how they are feeling about work and to build a shared understanding and a shared vision."

Although there is always initial resistance from at least a few staff members, United for Change has maintained its commitment to adult reflection for over seven years, since the practice was originally introduced to the school, because they see themselves as a learning organization engaged in a constant process of reflection and growth. Staff members reflect that the process nourishes them and allows them to work together as a team.

This is crucial, especially in the high-demand climate of public schooling, because it illuminates the understanding that adult reflection is indeed a vehicle for student success. In fact, schools that are engaged in the process of adult reflection point to it as a necessary element of professional development, one that keeps adults from distracting from the mission of their schools.

Cohesion is a key word that comes up again and again in conversations about adult reflection because in order to be able to give critical feedback and push one another, staff members must feel connected and build trust. Leon describes the role of adult reflection in helping him establish a relationship with his instructional coach, which allowed for challenging conversations around his classroom practice. "Peter was the coach that got me to buy into backward planning," Leon explains, "adjusting my pedagogy in ways that I would not have without that trust and relationship."

He goes on to describe how, over time and through the process of adult reflection, that trust deepened to the point where his coach could give him feedback on just about anything and he would take it as constructive and supportive. Peter challenged Leon to try hard to reach the four boys who sat in the back of his classroom disengaged. He pushed him to leverage his strong relationships with students to get more out of them academically; he even got Leon to take some leadership over the adult reflection process, as opposed to being the reluctant participant he was when he arrived at United for Change.

Both Leon and Katie added that the concrete skills of self-reflection, facilitation, and dialogue required for adult reflection are used in the classroom and even taught to students. Skills such as asking open-ended and empowering questions, making specific requests, challenging someone's ideas or words in a respectful way, self-management of emotions, noticing one's triggers, and setting growth goals all manifest on some level in every classroom at United for Change.

For the 2015–16 school year, adult reflection has been a particularly pertinent aspect of the school's professional development cycle. United for Change Charter High School experienced the highest rate of turnover it had since opening its doors in 2001. Over half the staff left the school at the end of the 2014–15 school year, including the two co-principals, Leon and Sharon, who have run the school together for five years.

Then, early in the new school year, the newly hired head principal left abruptly, creating a vacuum of leadership and further disrupting an already challenging year. Katie, the lead teacher who stepped up to take on many of the administrative responsibilities, insists how crucial it was that United for Change had the adult reflection process in place as they weathered this tumultuous time. "It created a sense of safety and helped us maintain a shared vision that was fundamental to the school regaining stability," she explains. "It was critical for supporting the building of our new team."

The first principle of restorative justice outlined in chapter 1 of this book asserts, "there must be a foundation of community." The adult reflection process comes from the recognition that a healthy, reflective, empowered adult community is absolutely necessary if we want the same to be true for our students and our schools as a whole. We can only expect of our students what we expect of ourselves.

ADULT RESTORATIVE CIRCLES

Tensions had been running high among the staff at East Bay Charter Academy in Oakland, California. The school had hired a new principal at the beginning of the year and she was proving to be highly competent in many ways, but also highly demanding and firmly set on her vision of school success. Her unrelenting pursuit of *her* vision created tension with several teachers at the school, some of whom had been putting their hearts and souls into East Bay Charter Academy's success for many years. Furthermore, several of the teachers on a staff comprised of about two-thirds educators of color felt that the new principal, who was white, did not demonstrate enough respect for the voices of staff of color and parents at a school with nearly 100 percent students of color.

The tension came to a head over a seemingly minor incident when several teachers, due to a miscommunication, returned late with their students from a school-sanctioned field trip, missing half of an afternoon professional development session. When the principal threatened to hold them one to two hours beyond the normal 4:30 conclusion of professional development, the room exploded into a dispute that resulted in multiple teachers walking out and, ultimately, the call to end the meeting early.

School leaders, both administrators and teachers, found themselves wondering what was next. They could not simply return to teaching and leading as usual and expect things to return to normal at professional development the following Wednesday. Some leaders called for the teachers who had walked out to be punished in some way. Others said that administration should apologize for threatening to keep teachers beyond their normal workday since they were late due to a school-sanctioned field trip. One teacher who had not walked out suggested mediation between the principal and several other teachers.

In the end, the leadership team realized that the disconnection was not simply the result of the field trip incident. Rather, it was the accumulation of conflicts and tensions that had been growing since the beginning of the year. In most of these cases, the conflicts involved the new principal—and her administrative team—and one or more teachers, with other staff members falling on both sides of the issue. It was apparent that trust and respect needed to be built, in some cases rebuilt, among the teachers and especially between teachers and administrators. Staff members needed to genuinely see, hear, and understand each other if East Bay Charter Academy was going to grow and flourish. The leadership team decided to engage in an adult restorative circle as a first step in this process.

While there is significant overlap between the purpose and focus of adult reflection and adult restorative circles, the main difference is that while adult reflection is an ongoing structure that takes place consistently over the course of a school year, or even multiple years, restorative circles can be either one-time or multiple-step activities in response to a specifically challenging or harmful incident. One does not replace the need for the other, and it might be the case that a school needs to implement both adult restorative circles and adult reflection in order to build a strong adult culture at the school.

Adult restorative circles follow the same process as student-focused circles. All impacted community members come together in a circle with the intention of restoring and transforming a conflict or incident of harm. In the case of East Bay Charter Academy, the group decided that the restorative circle should include all staff members because, regardless of their involvement in any of the conflicts or tensions since the beginning of the year, everyone was impacted by negative staff culture that was emerging. Additionally, because they recognized that any "requirement" communicated from the principal would be perceived by some as a top-down mandate, the school leadership team decided that the lead teachers would relate to the staff the restorative circle process.

Fortunately, the timing of the conflict over the field trip provided the leadership team several days to plan for the restorative process. The following Monday was a scheduled full day of professional development, and the staff felt like tending to adult relationships was a priority, so they rearranged the agenda to give the first three hours of time to the adult restorative circle.

Space is also a crucial consideration when engaging in an adult restorative circle. Classrooms and other spaces in schools can hold a great deal of symbolic meaning for teachers and staff, so it is important to select a space in which people feel like they can engage and open up in an authentic way. Leaders at East Bay Charter Academy chose to hold their restorative circle at a nearby community center because the space felt neutral to everyone. Being able to physically step into a different space reinforced the idea that the restorative circle held an alternative purpose to normal professional development.

To begin the restorative process and set expectations, the restorative justice facilitator asked all participants to write down on a piece of paper one intention and one fear they were bringing to the circle. After everyone had placed their papers in the middle of the circle, the facilitator discussed the issues that had created the need for the restorative process. Though she named the field trip conflict as the particular incident of harm, an incident that had felt damaging to both administrators and teachers, she made it clear that the restorative circle was meant to address broader tensions as well. She invited participants to speak their truths honestly and openly but also in ways that did not involve personal attacks toward others in the circle. After several minutes of framing the root causes of the conflict, she passed the talking stick to her right for the first teacher to share out.

With nearly thirty staff members participating in the circle, the first round of talking lasted well over an hour. Some staff members spoke only a few words while others shared for several minutes. Some spoke about how they felt like they were on the outside and relatively unaffected by the tensions, and others maintained that their health and well-being were being impacted significantly. Several staff members shed tears as they were speaking or listening to the words of others.

One powerful and *empowering* quality of circles is that they are egalitarian. Just like restorative structures such as circles and the Student Justice Panel changes the power dynamics between teachers and students, adult restorative circles change the power dynamics between teachers and administration. Multiple teachers used the space to share how they had struggled with what they perceived as an increasingly hierarchical structure at the school. Some also felt empowered, in a way they had never been before, to share directly with the new principal their concerns about her coming into the school community with a "savior" stance as opposed to one through which she viewed herself as a "servant leader."

Conversely, the principal discussed how she felt that she had never really been given a chance and had been excluded from the beginning by some staff members, making it practically impossible for her to be successful as a leader.

After the talking stick made one full revolution around the circle, allowing every participant a chance to share her or his truth, the facilitator opened the space for volunteers to continue speaking and to share anything they had not had time to share or thoughts that had come up during the first rotation.

The process continued for about another hour with participants offering general thoughts and feelings about the staff culture, as well as addressing other individuals in the circle about specific incidents. Occasionally, the facilitator asked specific questions of the group or pushed individual staff members to say more or clarify their points, but, for the most part, the second part of the sharing had an organic flow as the talking stick was passed randomly around the circle.

As the energy started to wane, the facilitator asked for final comments and reflections before closing the process by compelling the participants to carry their intentions forward and remember what was shared inside the circle as they moved back out to the craziness that is the daily life of an educator.

East Bay Charter Academy's adult restorative circle did accomplish the goal of helping staff members to see, hear, and understand each other more deeply than previous interactions had allowed. It was a humanizing process that did some work to shift the participants' perspectives of each other, both in the short term and the long term. However, it would be naïve to believe a restorative circle could change firmly entrenched relationship dynamics in a single bound. The school still had much work to do around cultural competence and difficult conversations regarding race. The same hierarchical structures that contributed to the initial conflict remained in place. Veteran teachers still held strongly to their vision of success for the school, even when the principal's leadership was producing results. Ultimately, the staff was compelled to engage in the process again in subsequent years as similar tensions and conflicts arose. But, fundamentally, what the adult restorative circle did accomplish was fostering enough space and goodwill for some of the more challenging ongoing conversations to happen in a productive way.

IT *IS* ABOUT THE STUDENTS

But there is just not enough time during the school day to work on adult relationships. This is the response of almost every educator contemplating engaging in structures such as adult reflection or adult restorative circles. It is a response that often reflects deep concern and a strong sense of urgency to support our students. We need to focus on literacy and numeracy instruction, cultural relevance, classroom management, backward unit planning, and, even if we do not like it, testing.

There is not enough time in the school day. Exactly—not enough time to be occupied by the tensions and conflicts that consume so much energy at schools with dysfunctional adult cultures. This is not the reality at every school, often either because teachers and school leaders have done the work to build respectful and humanizing adult cultures or because individuals in schools are so disconnected that they are doing their own thing in their classrooms or offices and not interacting enough to get in each other's ways. But in many schools, adult tensions and conflicts stand in the way of student success. In these cases, tending to adult relationship *is* in direct service to high expectations and rigor because if teachers cannot work together and support one another students suffer.

Rise Up High School and United for Change Charter School offer contrasting examples of how these adult restorative processes, or the lack thereof, impact time, resources, and energy in schools. United for Change, a school that has woven adult reflection into the fabric of their school culture responded to a tumultuous and stressful time by coming together and rebuilding a shared vision for the school. Rise Up, on the other hand, found that when tensions were high and staff members were feeling unsupported, a great deal of time and energy went into creating divisions and building up walls between teachers and administration. Restorative measures have been implemented in response to the divisions, but the process continues to be challenging due to the lack of a foundation of community.

LEADING THE WAY: HOLDING ADULTS TO THE SAME EXPECTATIONS AS STUDENTS

A widespread adage among the education community is that teachers make the worst students. We see this when teachers trickle in late or chomp down a burger and fries in a staff meeting after just having handed out detentions for tardies and eating in class; when they are asked to read an article silently during professional development and proceed to chat openly with their table partners; or when they miss another deadline to turn in that latest lesson plan. These are seemingly insubstantial examples, but they point to a real issue that schools struggle to address—adults must hold themselves to the same expectations to which they hold their students.

Conboy et al. (2004) point out the realization of this dilemma in their adult reflection work, "As adults challenged youth to consider thunderous concepts like 'rigor,' 'responsibility,' and 'authenticity,' they painfully discovered that no such expectations were being held for themselves" (1). These "thunderous concepts" lay the foundation for school culture and academic expectations and, for better and for worse, students look to the staff to model the kind of behavior and discipline they see as appropriate and acceptable.

When students experience teachers or administrators saying one thing but doing another, it negatively impacts school culture. When a teacher holds a hard line on a no-late-work policy but returns a graded essay two weeks after it was promised to the class, students grow frustrated with the hypocrisy. When schools implement strong policies regarding appropriate language while expletives fly freely among teachers, students begin to question the integrity of the staff. And when schools hold high expectations for students around core values like respect and growth, yet students see their teachers badmouthing their principal in the hallways or see the principal treating a teacher as inferior, they get the message that the school does not really mean what it says. This is a sure way to erode school culture and demean academic expectations.

Adult reflection and adult restorative circles are two structures that function to build, implement, and restore a respectful, productive, and humanizing adult culture, but staff members only engage in these processes once or twice per month, at most, and they require significant chunks of time outside of the school day to put it into effect with fidelity. Being a public school educator is an incredibly challenging vocation, and relationships in such an environment inevitably include tension and conflict. So, beyond the occasional structures like adult reflection and restorative circles, schools, if they wish to run smoothly and productively, must build in more ways to consistently tend to these relationships.

Many schools adopt norms to hold themselves accountable to a respectful, productive, and humanizing space, especially during difficult conversations or overwhelming situations. At East Bay Charter Academy and Rise Up High School, during professional development days at the beginning of the year, the entire staff would spend several hours developing, refining, and coming to agreement on a set of codes of respect (see appendix E) or staff norms (see appendix F) that were rooted in the school's core values.

Every staff meeting began by reading the school's core values and staff norms and ended with a process check connected to the same document. It was not uncommon for staff members to point out a staff norm that was being violated in a particularly tense circumstance. A teacher might point out to the principal, "It does not feel like you are being clear and transparent with us right now. Can you clarify and be specific about what you are asking us to do?" Grounding feedback in the staff norms allowed the recipients to hear it in a more open way because it was framed not as personal critique but as a transgression of guidelines to which they had agreed.

Educating young people requires a powerful sense of urgency. In many schools, this urgency can sideline the genuine need for adults to build and maintain healthy, respectful, and productive relationships with one another. When attempting to do restorative work with teachers and school leaders, the most common response is "we do not have time for that." Paradoxically, educators frequently respond in the same manner when encouraged to implement restorative practices with students.

These responses are understandable in the current context of public education. Teachers and school leaders are under immense pressure to perform and demonstrate results. And the work of restorative justice, either with staff or students, does not show up on any standard measures of accountability on which educators and students are being assessed. But we must ask ourselves—what is the true purpose of education in schools? If test scores and GPAs provide our only measure and we wish to continue to perpetuate the race- and class-based divisions that have historically defined schools, then restorative practices will remain on the margins. However, if our goal is to help young people realize healthy, empowered, and productive lives with a strong sense of community and possibility, restorative justice provides a valuable tool for doing that work. And adults must show them the way forward.

Appendix A

Sample Student Justice Panel Overview

The Student Justice Panel (SJP) is a restorative justice model of school discipline, the purpose of which is to uphold the school's core values by working to restore damaged relationships between individuals and the community. The SJP will be made up of elected student leaders and is based on the beliefs that:

- Our school believes strongly in maintaining our Core Values of Discipline, Growth, Community, Justice, and Respect
- Each individual at our school is responsible for the community as a whole
- Our school functions best when students take leadership and are given a strong voice

Because each individual is responsible for the success of all members of our community, justice begins with individuals acting as upstanders. Any member of the school community (student, teacher, or staff member) can and should request an SJP hearing if they believe the actions of another or others have violated the core values. The purpose of these hearings is to:

- Help members of the school community understand how their actions impact others
- Identify underlying actions that allowed such actions to occur
- Provide consequences that restore the community while reinstating in a just manner those who did the harm

SJP hearings consist of an adult facilitator, the community members involved in the violation of the core values, and at least four SJP representatives. Parents or family members may also be present, depending on need. Petitioners and respondents can also request to have additional student advocates present. Everyone at the hearing, including the respondent, will propose consequences aimed at restoration; consequences will be discussed and decided on by the SJP before being implemented.

The SJP model encourages all members of the school community to think critically, take responsibility, and get involved in upholding the core values in order to create and maintain a thriving school and develop empowered agents of change in our community and beyond.

STUDENT JUSTICE PANEL PROCEDURE

If you believe that the actions of another community member have detracted from your education and violated the school's core values, you can and should request a Student Justice Panel hearing.

Petitions

- Find an SJP petition in any classroom
- Thoughtfully and honestly complete the petition letter (if the petition is not thoughtful and thorough, it will be denied)
- Share the petition with the person or people you wish to bring before the SJP (if you need help or support in doing this, please discuss this with your advisor)
- Identify school staff to attend SJP (you must get at least one school staff member to attend in order have an SJP hearing)
- Submit the petition to the SJP coordinator by placing it in the SJP folder in the main office or by giving it to them directly

The SJP coordinator will review petitions and schedule hearings as appropriate.[1] The SJP will convene every other Monday during advisory and every Thursday after school, so you may be required to wait several days before the next SJP hearing. SJP hearings will consist of an adult facilitator, the community members involved in the violation of the core values, and at least four SJP representatives.

Opening

- The facilitator welcomes everyone, reviews the purpose of the SJP, and introduces the community members involved in the hearing

- The petitioner reads her or his petition letter to the group
- The respondent offers her or his reactions to the letter and reflects on her or his responsibility in the situation

Questioning

- The SJP representatives ask probing questions to determine the level of violation of the core values, to evaluate what relationships need to be restored, and to fully understand the underlying causes of the situation
- Petitioner and respondent respond to the questions

Consequences

- The respondent first suggests consequences aimed at restoring the community and addressing underlying causes
- SJP representatives suggest additional or revised consequences, again aimed at restoring the community and addressing underlying causes
- The respondent leaves the room while the SJP representatives discuss the suggested consequences and decide on which ones will be implemented
- The facilitator presents the consequences to the respondent, explains the rationale for choosing them, and officially puts them into effect

Closing

- The facilitator reviews the consequences to be enforced and the plan of action for holding the respondent and the SJP responsible for implementing them
- The facilitator assigns one SJP panel member as a liaison to make sure the consequences have been completed
- The facilitator thanks the SJP for their participation, the respondent for her or his cooperation, and the petitioner for her or his concern and willingness to take action to uphold the school core values

NOTE

1. Not all petitions that are submitted will lead to an SJP hearing. The SJP coordinator may recommend alternative solutions to the violation of core values.

Appendix B

Sample Student Justice Panel Petition

In order to be granted an SJP hearing, you must convince the committee that a conversation is necessary in order to repair one or more of the core values of community, discipline, respect, justice, and growth. Do this by writing a letter to the person or people you want to bring before the SJP that responds to the following prompts. If you are writing a letter on behalf of yourself in order to be granted an SJP hearing in the place of schoolwide discipline policies, you should address the letter to the SJP coordinator.

*If all consequences are not completed, Student Justice Plan is null and student receives punitive consequences based on discipline policy.

Student Name _____   Date: _____

Specifically describe the person's/people's behavior and actions:

_____

_____

_____

_____

_____

This behavior harmed the community because (describe the specific Core Value/s the behavior violated and how):

_____

_____

_____

_____

_____

_____

The steps I have already taken to address the situation are:

_____

_____

_____

_____

I am offering to further help the situation by:

_____

_____

Anything else I would like to say about the situation:

_____

_____

_____

_____

_____

Adult who will be attending Student Justice Panel hearing: _____

Signed: _____   Date: _____

>

Reviewed by _____

   ☐ SJP Hearing **Approved**

      Date of SJP Hearing _____

   ☐ SJP Hearing **Not Approved** because: _____

_____

*If approval not recommended, SJP coordinator must check in with SJP leaders

   ☐ All parties involved contacted about SJP hearing _____

   ☐ SJP Consequences:

      ☐ _____

      ☐ _____

      ☐ _____

   ☐ Student has completed all consequence actions and case is closed.*

Signed _____

Appendix C

Student Justice Panel Training

Time	Action	Purpose
9:00 – 9:45	Breakfast and community building • Social Justice Bingo • On My Island	Get nourished and connect with one another
9:45 – 10:15	Socratic Discussion - What is justice? • Write individual definitions of justice and share out • Gallery walk and comment on each others' definitions of justice • What does justice look like? What does it NOT look like? In the world? In Oakland? At EA?	Start to build a common understanding of how we define justice
10:15 – 11:15	Restorative Justice vs. Punitive Justice - Why restorative justice? • Definitions and Examples • Discussion - What is the purpose and value of each? • Historical Case Study - Video - Facing the Truth - Segment 7 (1:10:20 - 1:18:39) • Reading - "Opening Up" NY Times Article • Socratic discussion a) Do people need to be punished for breaking the law or hurting others? b) Does punishment change people's behavior? c) How is restorative justice different than punitive justice? d) Do you think restorative justice could make our society a better place? e) Do you think restorative justice could make EA a better school?	Build knowledge about restorative justice and how it is an entirely different paradigm than punitive justice
11:15 – 11:30	Break	
11:30 – 12:00	What is the SJP? How does it work? • Go over SJP Overview and discuss	Build an understanding of the technical aspects of the SJP and how the process works
12:00 – 12:45	Lunch	

12:45 – 1:45	Revising the process - student input • Review the SJP application and procedures and gather input from students • Brainstorm restorative consequences	Give voice to students to provide input for the SJP process; increase buy-in
1:45 – 2:30	SJP mock scenarios in small groups • Hand out one scenario at a time and ask students to work through how they would respond • For each scenario, groups should work through the following questions: A. Who are the stakeholders? B. What pre-conditions allowed this situation to develop? C. What additional information do you need to find out before responding appropriately? D. What are the implications of this situation for the teacher? The administrators? The student? Other students? E. What are the options that include a restorative justice component? F. What are the different goals that can be articulated in relation to this situation, from pre- to post?	Practice working together and using the SJP process
2:30 – 3:00	Questions, Props, Closing	

Time	Action	Purpose
9:00 – 9:30	Breakfast and community builder	Get nourished and connect with one another
9:30 – 10:15	Predicting the challenges • As a group, make a list of all the possible challenges and obstacles that will be encountered during the SJP process • In group of 3-4, brainstorm solutions	Make predictions and prepare for some of the challenges students will encounter
10:15 – 11:00	More SJP mock scenarios in new small groups • Hand out one scenario at a time and ask students to work through how they would respond • For each scenario, groups should work through the following questions: A. Who are the stakeholders? B. What pre-conditions allowed this situation to develop? C. What additional information do you need to find out before responding appropriately? D. What are the implications of this situation for the teacher? The administrators? The student? Other students? E. What are the options that include a restorative justice component? F. What are the different goals that can be articulated in relation to this situation, from pre- to post?	Practice working together and using the SJP process
11:00 – 12:00	Mock Student Justice Panel • Assign various roles to students and choose one of the scenarios you practiced • Run through the entire SJP process from beginning to end	Prepare for actual SJP process
12:00 – 12:30	Questions, Props, Closing	

Appendix D

Reflective Time

REFLECTIVE TIME

Name _____ Date _____ Advisor _____

Class you are leaving _____ Teacher Signature _____

We recognize there are times when students just need to take a moment to gather themselves and reflect outside of class. The purpose of Reflective Time is to allow you to do this in the safe space of your Advisor's classroom. YOU SHOULD BE GONE FROM CLASS NO MORE THAN 10 MINUTES. IF YOU ABUSE THIS PRIVILEGE IT WILL GO AWAY.

If you feel like you need to remove yourself from class, please follow these steps:

1. **Do not interrupt the teaching and learning that is happening in the class**
2. **Check in with your teacher about leaving the class**
3. **Take a Reflective Time form and fill out the top**
4. **Get your teacher to sign the form**
5. **Go directly to your Advisor (no stops by the bathroom, office, etc)**
6. **Enter your Advisors classroom quietly**
7. **Find an open seat away from distractions**
8. **Fill out the Reflective Time form**
9. **If necessary, check in briefly with your Advisor (but do not interrupt the teaching and learning that is happening in this class)**
10. **Return to class**

Directions: Please answer the following questions thoughtfully and honestly.

1. What's going on? Why do you need a break from class right now?

_____

_____

_____

_____

_____

_____

2. What do you need right now to be able to get back to learning? What can your Advisor do to support you? What can your teacher do to support you?

   _____

   _____

   _____

   _____

   _____

   _____

3. What can you do differently next time in order to not miss out on your learning?

   _____

   _____

   _____

4. Do you feel like you need to set up a meeting to resolve an issue or problem? Yes No

   When would you like to meet with staff and/or student involved to resolve the issue.

   _____ (day) at _____ (time)

   _____   _____   _____ _____
   Student Signature   Advisor Signature   Date   Time

Appendix E

Adult Professional Learning Community

CODES OF RESPECT AGREEMENTS

Respect Self	Respect Words
We start and end on time.	We use a tone of voice and language-choice that is positive encouraging, and empowering.
We stay focused, productive, and make thoughtful choices that bring success to everyone.	We use respectful language, assume best intentions, and ask for clarification: communicating openly and mindfully.
We recognize we're always learning and growing.	We start with inquiry and positivity.
We love ourselves and protect our reputations.	We are asset-based in our conversation, particularly with student-talk.
Instructional Leaders prepare engaging and illuminating professional development, consistently and ahead of time.	

Respect Space	Respect Others
We clean up after ourselves, keep our shared space organized, and step up to keep our space beautiful and productive.	We share one mic, we listen attentively, we respectfully disagree, and we accept each other's uniqueness.
We recognize that this is a shared space of learning and we all contribute to its success.	We treat others like they'd like to be treated.
We understand the value of setting aside time for professional development.	We adopt a collaborative stance and co-create our learning space.
	We trust our colleagues, treat them equitably, and support each other to reach individual & collective goals.

Appendix F

Sample Core Values and Staff Norms

RESPECT: WE SEEK TO SEE THE BEST IN EACH OTHER AND TREAT ONE ANOTHER WITH DIGNITY. WE GIVE RESPECT IN ORDER TO GET RESPECT.

- We respect the expertise, experiences, and differences of every team member.
- We believe every team member is good, wise, and powerful.
- We are clear and transparent.
- We avoid gossiping and talking behind others' backs in order to maintain an honest and respectful community. We check each other when appropriate.

DISCIPLINE: WE DISCIPLINE OURSELVES, SO THAT NO ONE ELSE HAS TO.

- We are professional and stay present by demonstrating mental and physical focus to the task at hand.
- We clearly communicate deadlines and expectations, giving sufficient time to complete tasks. We meet deadlines, follow-through on commitments, and communicate ahead of time if challenges arise.

GROWTH: WE ARE COMMITTED TO LIFELONG LEARNING AND PERSONAL GROWTH .

- We hold ourselves and the Envision Academy community to unified high expectations in the best interest of students.
- We push and expect to be pushed on our knowledge, skills, and mindsets.
- We acknowledge that intention and impact are not the same and, therefore, take responsibility for our impact as well as our intentions.

COMMUNITY: WE WORK HARD AND TAKE RESPONSIBILITY FOR THE SUCCESS OF ALL COMMUNITY MEMBERS .

- We listen in order to understand.
- We discuss issues and conflicts with a focus on resolution.
- We use joy and food to strengthen our community.

JUSTICE: WE ARE EMPOWERED AGENTS OF CHANGE FOR EQUITY AND SOCIAL JUSTICE.

- We speak our truth, and space is given to do so.
- We are mindful that our language (including body language) and actions reflect our beliefs.
- We actively advocate for decisions and actions that are just and equitable and root our decision making in the experiences and needs of our families and the communities in which they live.
- We are prepared to confront the inequalities woven into our social fabric; therefore, we educate in order to develop students' academic and social-emotional skills, so they are prepared to face the inequity they will encounter in the world.

This is a living document. We will check in on our staff norms based on our core values as needed.

As a staff, we will undergo a self-assessment of staff norms based on our core values during the year to encourage mindfulness.

References

Adams, Erica J. 2010. "Healing Invisible Wounds: Why Investing in Trauma-Informed Care for Children Makes Sense." *Justice Policy Institute*. July: 1-15.

Alexander, Michelle. 2010. *The New Jim Crow: Mass Incarceration in and Age of Colorblindness*. New York: The New Press.

Alfred, Renjitham, and Jon Kidde. 2011. *Restorative Justice: A Working Guide for Our Schools*. Alameda County School Health Services Coalition.

Amstutz, Lorraine Stutzman, and Judy H. Mullet. 2005. *The Little Book of Restorative Discipline for Schools: Teaching Responsibility; Creating Caring Climates*. Pennsylvania: Good Books.

Ashley, Jessica, and Kimberly Burke. *Implement Restorative Justice: A Guide for Schools*. Chicago, IL: Illinois Criminal Justice Information Authority.

Ayers, W., B. Dohrn, and R. Ayers. 2001. *Zero Tolerance: Resisting the Drive for Punishment in Our Schools: A Handbook for Parents, Students, Educators, and Citizens*. New York: New Press.

Bickmore, Kathy. 2005. "Teacher Development for Conflict Participation: Facilitating Learning for 'Difficult Citizenship' Education." *International Journal of Citizenship and Teacher Education*. 1(2), http//:www.citized.info.

Black Organizing Project, Public Counsel, ACLU. 2013. *From Report Card to Criminal Record: The Impact of Policing Oakland Youth*. http://www.publiccounsel.org/tools/assets/files/0436.pdf.

Bowles, Samuel, and Herbert Gintis. 1976. *Schooling in Capitalist America: Educational Reform and the Contradictions of Economic Life*. New York: Basic.

Braithwaite, John. 2002. *Restorative Justice and Responsive Regulation*. Oxford University Press: New York.

Clark, Kenneth B. 1965. *Dark Ghetto: Dilemmas of Social Power*. New York: Harper.

Claassen, Ron and Roxanne Claassen. 2008. *Discipline that Restores: Strategies to Create Respect, Cooperation, and Responsibility in the Classroom*. South Carolina: BookSurge Publishing.

Coates, Ta-Nehisi. 2015. *Between the World and Me*. New York: Spiegel & Grau.

Conboy, Edd. *Alternatives in Action and On the Move*. 2004. Adult Reflection Elements

Devine, John. 1996. *Maximum Security: The Culture of Violence in Inner-City Schools*. University of Chicago Press.

Edelman, M. W. (2007) "The Cradle to Prison Pipeline: An American Health Crisis." *Preventing Chronic Disease* 4 (3): 1–2.

Fabelo, Tony, et al. 2011. *Breaking Schools' Rules: A Statewide Study of How School Discipline Relates to Students' Success and Juvenile Justice Involvement*. New York: The Coun-

cil of State Governments Justice Center and the Public Policy Research Institute, Texas A&
M University.

Fagan, J. (2002). "Policing Guns and Youth Violence." *The Future of Children* 12 (2):
133–151.

Feld, Barry C. 1998. "Juvenile and Criminal Justice Systems' Responses to Youth Violence."
In *Crime and Justice: A Review of Research: Youth Violence* Vol. 24, edited by Michael
Tonry and Mark H. Moore. Chicago: University of Chicago Press.

Gillen, Jay. 2014. *Educating for Insurgency: The Roles of Young People in Schools of Poverty.*
Oakland: AK Press.

Gilmore, Ruth Wilson. 2007. *Golden Gulag: Prisons, Surplus, Crisis, and Opposition in Glo-
balizing California.* Berkeley: University of California Press.

———. 2008. "Forgotten Places and the Seeds of Grassroots Planning." In *Engaging Contradictions: Theory, Politics, and Methods of Activist Scholarship* 1st ed., edited by C. R. Hale,
31–61. Berkeley: University of California Press. Retrieved from http://www.jstor.org/stable/
10.1525/j.ctt1pncnt.7.

———. 2007. "In the Shadow of the Shadow State." In *The Revolution Will Not Be Funded:
Beyond the Non-Profit Industrial Complex.* Editor INCITE! Women of Color Against Violence. Cambridge, MA: South End Press.

Greene, Ross W. 2008. *Lost at School: Why Our Kids with Behavioral Challenges Are Falling
through the Cracks and How We Can Help Them.* New York: Scribner.

Gregory, Anne, Russell J. Skiba, and Pedro A. Noguera. 2010. "The Achievement Gap and the
Discipline Gap: Two Sides of the Same Coin?" *Educational Researcher* 39 (1): 59–68.

Hammond, Zaretta. 2014. *Culturally Responsive Teaching and the Brain: Promoting Authentic
Engagement and Rigor among Culturally and Linguistically Diverse Students.* Thousand
Oaks: Corwin.

Harvey, D. 2005. *A Brief History of Neoliberalism.* Oxford: Oxford University Press.

Heifetz, Ronald A., and Martin Linsky. 2002. *Leadership on the Line: Staying Alive through
the Dangers of Leading.* Boston: Harvard Business School Publishing.

Hopkins, Belinda. 2003. "Restorative Justice in Schools." *Support for Learning* 17: 144-149.

———. 2014. "Incarceration Nation." *American Psychological Association* 45 (9). Accessed
January 30, 2016.

INCITE! Women of Color Against Violence. 2007. "The Revolution Will Not Be Funded :
Beyond the Non-profit Industrial Complex." Cambridge, Mass: South End Press.

Jain, Sonia, Henrissa Bassey, Martha A. Brown, and Preety Kalra. 2014. *Restorative Justice in
Oakland Schools: Implementation and Impacts.* Oakland: Oakland Unified School District.

Kidde J., and A. Alfred. 2011. *Restorative Justice: A Working Guide for Our Schools.* Alameda, CA: Alameda County School Health Services Coalition.

Kohl, Herbert. 1992. "I Won't Learn from You! Thoughts on the Role of Assent in Learning."
Rethinking Schools 7: 16–19.

Kohl, Herbert. 1994. *I Won't Learn from You: And Other Thoughts on Creative Maladjustment.*
New York: The New Press.

Krisberg, Barry. 2005. *Juvenile Justice: Redeeming Our Children.* Thousand Oaks, CA: Sage
Publications.

Laura, Crystal T. 2014. *Being Bad: My Baby Brother and the School-to-Prison Pipeline.* New
York: Teachers College Press.

Lewis, Katherine Reynolds. 2015. "What If Everything You Knew About Disciplining Kids
Was Wrong?" *Mother Jones* July/August.

Losen, Daniel, Cheri Hodson, Michael A. Keith, II, Katrina Morrison, and Shakti Belway.
2015. *Are We Closing the School Discipline Gap?* Los Angeles: UCLA Center for Civil
Rights Remedies.

Losen, Daniel J., and Daniel Gillespe. 2012. *Opportunities Suspended: The Disparate Impact
of Disciplinary Suspension for School.* Los Angeles: UCLA Center for Civil Rights Remedies.

Losen, Daniel J., and Tia Elena Martinez. 2013. *Out of School and Off Track: The Overuse of
Suspension in American Middle Schools and High Schools.* Los Angeles: UCLA Center for
Civil Rights Remedies.

McCaslin, Wanda D., ed. 2005. *Justice as Healing—Indigenous Ways: Writings on Community Peacemaking and Restorative Justice from the Native Law Centre.* St. Paul: Living Justice Press.

Mergler, Mary Schmidt, Karla M. Vargas, and Caroline Caldwell. 2014. "Alternative Discipline Can Benefit Learning." *Phi Delta Kappan* 96: 25–30.

Morris, Ruth. 2000. *Stories of Transformative Justice.* Toronto: Canadian Scholar's Press.

Morrison, Brenda E. and Dorothy Vaandering. 2012. "Restorative Justice: Pedagogy, Praxis, and Discipline." *Journal of School Violence* 11: 138–155.

Morrison, Brenda. 2007. *Restoring Safe School Communities.* Leichhardt, NSW: Federation Press.

Morrison, B., P. Blood, and M. Thorsborne. 2005. "Practicing Restorative Justice in School Communities." *Public Organization Review: A Global Journal* 5: 335–356.

National Center for Education Statistics. "Public High School Graduation Rates." Last modified May 2015. http://nces.ed.gov/programs/coe/indicator_coi.asp.

Nocella II, Anthony J., Priya Parmar, and David Stovall. 2014. *From Education to Incarceration: Dismantling the School-to-Prison Pipeline.* New York: Peter Lang Publishing.

Payne, Allison Ann and Kelly Welch. 2013. "Restorative Justice in Schools: The Influence of Race on Restorative Discipline." *Youth & Society.*

Perlstein, D. 1990. "Teaching Freedom: SNCC and the Creation of the Mississippi Freedom Schools." *History of Education Quarterly* 30 (3): 297–324.

Prothrow-Stith, Deborah and Howard R. Spivak. 2004. *Murder Is No Accident: Understanding and Preventing Youth Violence in America.* San Francisco: Jossey-Bass.

Rios, Victor. 2011. *Punished: Policing the Lives of Black and Latino Boys.* New York: New York University Press.

Roth, G., A. Assor, C. P. Niemiec, R. M. Ryan, and E. L. Deci. 2009. "The Emotional and Academic Consequences of Parental Conditional Regard: Comparing Conditional Positive Regard, Conditional Negative Regard, and the Autonomy Support as Parenting Practices." *Developmental Psychology* 45: 1119–1142.

Skiba, R. J. and K. Knesting. 2002 . "Zero Tolerance, Zero Evidence: An Analysis of School Disciplinary Practice." In *New Directions for Youth Development*, Edited by J. Skiba and G. G. Noam, 17–43. San Francisco: Jossey-Bass.

Skiba, Russel, et al. 2006. *Are Zero Tolerance Policies Effective in Schools? An Evidentiary Review and Recommendations.* Washington, DC: American Psychological Association Zero Tolerance Task Force.

Skiba, Russell, Robert S. Michael, Abra Carroll Nardo, and Reece L. Peterson. 2002. "The Color of Discipline: Sources of Racial and Gender Disproportionality in School Punishment." *The Urban Review* 34 (4): 317–342.

Skiba, Russell. 2000. *Zero Tolerance, Zero Evidence: An Analysis of School Disciplinary Practice.* Policy Research Report #SRS2. Bloomington, IN: Indiana Education Policy Center.

Smith, E. J., and S. R. Harper. 2015. "Disproportionate Impact of K–12 School Suspension and Expulsion on Black Students in Southern States." Philadelphia: University of Pennsylvania, Center for the Study of Race and Equity in Education.

Stinchcomb, J. B., G. Bazemore, and N. Riestenberg. 2006. "Beyond Zero Tolerance: Restoring Justice in Secondary Schools." *Youth Violence and Juvenile Justice* 4: 123–147. doi:10.1177/1541204006286287.

Strom, Margot S. 1994. *Facing History and Ourselves: Holocaust and Human Behavior: Resource Book.* Brookline, MA: Facing History and Ourselves National Foundation.

Sumner, Michael D., Carols J. Silverman, and Mary Louise Frampton. 2010. *School-Based Restorative Justice as an Alternative to Zero-Tolerance Policies: Lessons from West Oakland.* Berkeley: Thelton E. Henderson Center for Social Justice.

Tagaki, Paul, and Gregory Shank. 2004. "Critique of Restorative Justice." *Social Justice* 31: 147–163.

Thorsborne, Margaret and Peta Blood. 2013. *Implementing Restorative Practices in Schools: A Practical Guide to Transforming School Communities.* London: Jessica Kingsley Publishers.

Van Ness, Daniel W. and Karen Armstrong. 2015. *Restoring Justice: An Introduction to Restorative Justice*. New York: Routledge.

Wadhwa, A. 2016. *Restorative Justice in Urban Schools: Disrupting the School-to-prison Pipeline*. New York: Routledge.

Watkins, W. H. 1994. "Multicultural Education: Toward a Historical and Political Inquiry." *Educational Theory* 44: 99–116. doi: 10.1111/j.1741-5446.1994.00099.x.

———. 2012. *The Assault on Public Education: Confronting the Politics of Corporate School Reform*. New York: Teachers College Press.

Yang, K. Wayne. 2009. "Discipline or Punish: Some Suggestions for School Policy and Teacher Practice." *Language Arts* 87 (1): 49–61.

Zehr, Howard. 2002. *The Little Book of Restorative Justice*. Intercourse, PA: Goodbooks.

About the Author

Trevor W. Gardner has taught high school English and history for the past seventeen years in San Francisco and Oakland, where he has practiced and studied the use of restorative justice in urban schools. He currently teaches history and serves as the Dean of Instruction and Academic Coach at ARISE High School in East Oakland. Gardner has worked extensively with organizations such as Youth Speaks, Voice of Witness, and Facing History and Ourselves, where he serves on their Innovative Schools Network Advisory Board. He lives in Oakland, California, with his life-partner, Shikira, and their son, Omari. This is his first book.

About the Contributors

Renjitham Alfred has dedicated many years to serving youth and families in the Bay Area. She started her career in restorative justice as the Restorative Justice Coordinator at Cole Middle School in West Oakland and later with Restorative Justice for Oakland Youth. She interfaced with various system stakeholders, including school site and district administration, teachers, students, and families, school and city police, and community-based organizations, to lead a successful program. This pilot program was so effective in reducing suspensions, expulsions, and violence that staff at approximately twenty additional schools sought training and technical assistance to bring restorative practices to their sites. Rita and others assisted the OUSD School Board to pass a resolution adopting restorative justice districtwide as official policy. Since that time, Rita has trained over 3,000 people in schools, coached, and consulted with four school districts to adopt restorative justice practices at their schools. She is a founder of Restorative Justice Training Institute and continues in school-based restorative justice work as trainer, coach, and consultant. She has two sons and two grandchildren and lives in the Bay Area.

Jeremiah Jeffries is one of the main coordinators for Teachers 4 Social Justice (www.t4sj.org), a grassroots professional development organization focused on training teachers to create empowering learning environments. He is an education activist focused on changing education policy to better serve public school children. He has been teaching for over seventeen years and currently teaches first grade at Redding Elementary in San Francisco and works as adjunct faculty in the Teacher Education Department at the University of San Francisco. He serves as the founding board president for the Center for Critical Environmental Global Literacy (www.ccegl.org), training educators to build environmental justice education in their practice and work with educators internationally. He also facilitates professional development, trainings, and workshops on school climate, student discipline, classroom management, restorative practices, and parenting for success in public schools.

Rekia Jibrin is a teacher and scholar whose work focuses on race, class, and criminalization in schooling. Rekia conducted a three-year qualitative evaluation of restorative justice in a Bay Area high school. Her current research focuses on restorative justice, race, and questions of poverty in American public schools.

Milton Reynolds is a San Francisco Bay Area–based career educator and activist. His activism has been devoted to juvenile justice reform and law enforcement accountability. In support of these efforts Milton served twelve years as a commissioner on the San Mateo County Juvenile Justice and Delinquency Prevention Commission and was one of the founding members of the Racial Justice Coalition, an organization created to mobilize community in support of a law enforcement data collection bill to end the practice of racial profiling in California.

Since 2002, Milton has served as the board chair of Literacy for Environmental Justice (LEJ) a Bayview/Hunters Point-based nonprofit organization focused on youth leadership development and addressing the legacies of environmental racism in the Southeast of San Francisco. LEJ is currently leading the largest wetlands restoration project in the history of San Francisco.

Milton also sits on the advisory board of the Paul K. Longmore Institute on Disability at San Francisco State University. Part think-tank, part cultural center, the Paul K. Longmore Institute on Disability introduces new ideas about disability and disabled people.

Milton has served as a middle school self-science instructor for the past twenty-four years. Before his current position, he was one of the founders and the curriculum design specialist for CoAction, an equity and communications consulting firm. Additionally, he was a researcher in the Stanford Integrated Schools Project, a Stanford University–based research investigation designed to determine whether there were classroom practices educators could implement that would reduce or eliminate stereotype threat.

Currently, Milton is a senior program associate with Facing History and Ourselves. His work with Facing History and Ourselves has been largely focused on providing professional development for teachers in deepening their classroom implementation of the *Race and Membership in American History: The Eugenics Movement* resource book. The book is a case study developed for classroom use and is focused on four domains of eugenic policy influence including education, immigration, marriage restriction, and sterilization.